Good Housekeeping

·············· the ··············

Great
POTLUCK
COOKBOOK

··

Our Favorite Recipes for
Carry-In Suppers, Brunch Buffets,
Tailgate Parties & More!

HEARST BOOKS
A division of Sterling Publishing Co., Inc.

New York / London
www.sterlingpublishing.com

GOOD HOUSEKEEPING

Rosemary Ellis	Editor in Chief
Sara Lyle	Lifestyle Director
Susan Westmoreland	Food Director
Samantha B. Cassetty, MS, RD	Nutrition Director
Sharon Franke	Kitchen Appliances and Technology Director

Editor: Pam Hoenig
Production editor: Sarah Scheffel
Photography Credits on page 176

Library of Congress Cataloging-in-Publication Data

Good housekeeping the great potluck cookbook : our favorite recipes for carry-in suppers, brunch buffets, tailgate parties & more!.
    p. cm.
  Includes index.
1. Cooking, American. I. Hearst Books (Firm) II. Good housekeeping. III. Title: Great potluck cookbook.
  TX715.G6255 2011
  641.5973—dc22

                        2010028941

10 9 8 7 6 5 4 3 2 1

641.5973
GRE

Published by Hearst Books
A division of Sterling Publishing Co., Inc.
387 Park Avenue South, New York, NY 10016

Good Housekeeping is a registered trademark of Hearst Communications, Inc.

www.goodhousekeeping.com

For information about custom editions, special sales, premium and corporate purchases, please contact Sterling Special Sales Department at 800-805-5489 or specialsales@sterlingpublishing.com.

Distributed in Canada by Sterling Publishing
c/o Canadian Manda Group
165 Dufferin Street
Toronto, Ontario, Canada M6K 3H6

Distributed in Australia by Capricorn Link (Australia) Pty. Ltd.
P.O. Box 704, Windsor, NSW 2756 Australia

Manufactured in China

Sterling ISBN 978-1-58816-827-6

Contents

Garden-Fresh Chopped Salad with Herb-Ranch Dressing (recipe page 76)

Foreword

These days we're all looking for relaxed, cozy ways to gather friends and family without the cost (or formality) of a restaurant meal. Potluck parties, whether they be picnics, buffets, tailgates, or other "bring-a-dish" gatherings fit the bill perfectly. Long a staple of large family get togethers and community group fundraisers, potluck parties have become an increasingly popular way to entertain small or large groups. Whether at home or in the park, the host coordinates the menu, then everyone brings a dish—it's communal dining at its very best!

To make your potluck come off without a hitch, *The Great Potluck Cookbook* opens with organizing basics. You'll learn how to plan a menu and assign dishes, choose a fun theme and pick the perfect venue, pack and transport food safely, and set up an attractive buffet. Then it's on to the recipes: We've made it a snap to organize great potluck celebrations year-round by providing ten seasonal menus with dishes tailored to each event. From a Mother's Day Brunch to a Potluck Patio Party, a Super Bowl Shindig and a Day After Thanksgiving Dinner Party, our festive, easy-to-execute menus make throwing a potluck as enjoyable for the host as it is for the guests.

Celebrate your annual family reunion with our down-home picnic featuring grab-and-go appetizers, three kinds of succulent barbecue, refreshing salads, and PB&J and S'mores Bars for a sweet finale. When summer turns to autumn, throw together a tailgate party: Our menu includes Easy Spicy Cheese Straws and other yummy nibbles, hearty entrées like Salsa Verde Enchiladas, plus Hot Mulled Wine and Spiced Cider to keep everyone warm and cozy.

Throughout the book, you'll find Potluck Prep tips that offer advice on preparing dishes ahead and how to get them to your destination in party-perfect form. Plus, as a bonus, in the back of the book, you'll find perforated tabletop cards, so you can dress up your buffet table with the names of all the tempting dishes and their proud creators. It's a great reminder about the first rule of potlucking: Get everyone in on the act!

Susan Westmoreland
Food Director, *Good Housekeeping*

Introduction

Today, with time and money at a premium for most all of us, potluck is the perfect way to entertain. And if you've thought of potlucking but maybe felt uncomfortable asking people to contribute a dish, don't. Once you get over the hump of organizing your first potluck, you'll find that your friends will be delighted to participate and will be happy to take direction regarding what to make. One of the real benefits of potlucking is that because entertaining becomes so much easier, you'll find

yourself doing it with greater frequency. You could start a potluck round robin, with your circle of friends and family taking turns hosting.

POTLUCK 101

A successful potluck requires just a little prior thought and preparation. If you're throwing your first potluck, there are few things you'll want to consider:

1 WHAT YOUR MENU WILL BE. We've helped you out on this count by providing recipes for ten seasonal menus. Pick a party and you're ready to go—all you need to do is copy and hand out the recipes. Or you can create your own potluck menu, pulling together recipes that seem like they would work well together. The other option is to decide what you would like to prepare (say, a glazed ham), then enlist your guests for the rest, asking them to bring an appetizer, side dish, additional main course, or dessert that they think would work with your dish. This option adds an element of surprise to the get-together, plus it gives your guests the opportunity to share some of their favorite recipes.

Also, when selecting a menu, consider your guests and their eating habits. If you know you've got a vegetarian or someone with a specific food allergy coming, make sure to select an appetizer and dessert that everyone can enjoy and be sure there is at least one main course they can eat.

2 HOW TO ASSIGN DISHES. By all means, if you have a friend who is a dynamite baker, sign her up for dessert. If you've enjoyed a particular dish at a friend's house, don't be shy about asking him to prepare it. And if one or several guests don't have the strongest cooking skills, asking them to prepare a recipe you supply them with might be the best way to go; be sure to give them one suited to their skills.

3 HOW YOU WILL SERVE. For a potluck, you'll either want to serve family style, setting all the dishes out on the table for your guests to help themselves once they are seated, or buffet style. For a buffet, consider how you are going to keep hot foods hot and cold foods cold. If your guests don't bring their contributions in insulated food carriers or coolers, perishable cold foods should be stored in the fridge until serving time. Hot foods may need a quick stovetop simmer or pop in the oven to warm them up to the correct serving temperature before setting them out. If you think you might be potlucking on a regular basis, consider investing in several chafing dishes or insulated stainless steel–lined covered serving dishes. If you have a group you potluck with regularly, each of you could purchase a chafing dish and bring it to the parties.

The Entertaining Slow Cooker

The slow cooker is indispensable for no-fuss everyday meals, but it's also a great tool for the buffet table. It's perfect for keeping soups, stews, braises (like our Hungarian Veal Goulash on page 166), or chili at a satisfying simmer for up to two hours (use the Low or Keep Warm setting). There is even a mini slow cooker available, tailor made for hot dips (like the Hot Crabmeat Spread on page 136). Your slow cooker can also double as an electric punch bowl, keeping hot drinks hot, like our Warm Spiced Cider (page 101) and Hot Mulled Wine (page 100). Just set a ladle next to it and guests can serve themselves.

And remember, don't let food sit out at room temperature for more than two hours, including car time and sitting out for service.

IF YOU ARE BRINGING FOOD

The recipes in this book all contain Potluck Prep notes, advising you on how best to prepare and transport the dish to the potluck. Here are some additional tips for getting your contribution to its destination safe and sound.

Cover it well

- If your serving dish or bakeware doesn't come with a lid, make sure your casserole is securely wrapped. Cover it with a layer of plastic wrap, then a layer of foil. If you think there's still a chance the serving dish may leak, place it, with some absorbent paper underneath (newspaper works well), on a rimmed baking sheet or set it inside a cardboard box.

- If you are transporting a slow cooker, you can secure the lid by wrapping a rubber band around the handles.

- Be sure to set your dish (or slow cooker) on a flat surface in the car and position or bolster it in such a way that it won't tip over or slide around.

- Self-sealing plastic bags are great for toting foods such as crudités and garnishes. If you are transporting meat or poultry in marinade (for a grilling potluck, for instance), you might want to double-bag it to avoid leakage.

- There are all sorts of carriers available now designed especially for potlucks to keep foods from getting mangled in transit—carriers for deviled eggs, cupcakes, pies, and much more. The Internet is a great way to explore what's available.

Keep it cold (or hot)

- If you're bringing a cold dish that contains cooked meat, poultry, or seafood, make sure to refrigerate it until it is thoroughly chilled before packing it in a cooler.

- If you're bringing a hot dish, cook or reheat it fully right before leaving, then cover it securely. If you don't have a food carrier, you can wrap it in several layers of clean thick towels or newspaper to conserve heat. If you will be traveling some distance, you may need to reheat it at the potluck.

- There is a wide range of insulated food carriers available, from casserole carriers to insulated travel bags for slow cookers, that will keep your food at temperature for several hours, plus allow you to conveniently transport your dish.

Be on time

- If you're bringing an appetizer, be sure to arrive right on time or even 15 minutes early, particularly if you are the only person bringing an hors d'oeuvre.

Bring it ready to serve

- Being a good potlucker means bringing your dish ready to go, meaning in an attractive serving bowl, baking dish, platter, or cookware (like an enameled cast-iron Dutch oven) along with an appropriate serving utensil.

The Hostess with the Potluck Mostest

If you're throwing your first potluck, here are some tips for making it a hit.

- Think through your menu and be clear about assignments, including giving your dish-toting guests an idea of about how much to bring of whatever they're preparing. Although it's tempting to say, "Oh, bring whatever you'd like to make," that can result in three different guests walking through the door with bean dip. Assign guests a type of dish (an appetizer, side, dessert) and, if you are not giving them a recipe to prepare, make sure you check back a week before the potluck to find out what they are planning on bringing so you can do any necessary menu tweaking.

- Once you know what everyone is bringing, decide how it will be served. Will you be using disposable plates, glasses, and utensils? If not, do you have enough appropriate tableware? If you don't, confer with your guests in advance and see if they can supply what you are lacking.

- Before your guests arrive, if you will be serving buffet style, be sure to have the serving area cleared and ready to go. If any of your guests will be bringing a slow cooker, have an extension cord plugged in and at the ready (slow cookers always have short cords).

- Write the names of all the dishes that will be served on small cards folded like tents, so your guests will know what they're serving themselves. It would also be helpful to label those dishes that are vegetarian or vegan or to indicate items that contain ingredients that might be problematic for some of your guests (for example, dairy products, wheat products, nuts). For your convenience, we've provided attractive tear-out tabletop tents in the back of this book for this purpose.

- Before your guests arrive, turn your oven on low and, if you have one, turn on your warming drawer so you can keep hot foods hot while you enjoy a pre-meal cocktail and nibble.

- In a perfect world, it would be wonderful to hand your potluckers back clean dishes to take home. If that's not possible, at the very least be sure to rinse dishes out to avoid a messy ride home.

- If you decide it's preferable to assemble your dish at the potluck, make sure your host is aware that you'll be doing this and bring everything you'll need to put it together, including a knife and cutting board, if appropriate.

- In some cases, you might even want to bring the cup, bowl, or plate the drink or dish is to be served in. Say, for example, you're bringing punch. If you've got a punch bowl and punch cups, it makes sense for you to bring them. The same applies if you have a set of chili bowls or demitasse cups that would be perfect for serving a first-course soup. Confer with your host before the potluck to see whether bringing your own might be the way to go.

WHEN YOUR POTLUCK IS A PICNIC

Picnics require an extra level of planning, because you must bring everything you need with you—plates, utensils, cups, charcoal, lighter fluid, a portable grill if your picnic location doesn't have one, utensils for cooking and serving, platters, and much more. Antibacterial gel is also a good idea, particularly if your hands come into contact with raw meat. So is bug spray—nothing puts a damper on a picnic quicker than being attacked by mosquitoes. If you're going to be picnicking in a spot with no running water, you also might want to carry in several gallons of water. If you're picnicking out on a lawn, you'll want to bring either a blanket or folding chairs.

Picnicking in Style

A picnic can be as casual or as stylish as you want it to be. There is a wonderful history of dining outdoors in elegance, when people of means would have tables and chairs set up in bucolic environs and enjoy a selection of delicacies that had been packed into baskets for them.

Those days may be gone, but it's not that difficult to re-create the feeling. There are all sorts of lightweight collapsible chairs and tables available now that are easy to transport. And nothing makes a picnic more special than enjoying your food served on a real plate and sipping a cold glass of wine from a real glass. To make transporting your plates, utensils, and glasses to the picnic location of your choice easier, check the Internet for the numerous picnic backpacks now available, as well as other sorts of carriers.

Picnic Chicken Salad with Maple Vinaigrette (recipe page 91)

Spiced Kielbasa and Summer Fruit Kabobs (recipe page 45)

And don't forget clean-up: Unless the area is equipped with garbage cans and recycling bins, you've got to carry everything back out with you, so be sure to bring garbage bags, as well as paper towels and hand wipes to deal with spills, sticky barbecue hands, and charcoal smudges. Take the time to think it all through systematically—there is nothing worse than getting to a location, unpacking, settling in, and then realizing you haven't got matches, or a cork-screw, or a spatula to flip those sizzling burgers.

Once you've got your menu and your supplies list, you can divvy everything up between your guests. For a pre-concert picnic, you might want to go a little elegant and opt for real plates, wineglasses, and utensils. In that case, it makes sense for everyone to be responsible for their own table- and glassware. With a big picnic at a local park, paper plates and plastic cups are more the order and they can be assigned to someone to bring.

If you're throwing a big summertime bash or family reunion party, local state, town, and county parks often offer great facilities, whether your event is for family or friends. Groupings of picnic tables, multiple stand-up grills, playing fields, and swimming areas are just some of the amenities you can take advantage of. Be sure to call in advance to check on availability and reserve a spot if possible.

For a large potluck barbecue that is going to last several hours and where there is no available refrigeration, you want to avoid dealing with uncooked meat and poultry. You don't want your grillmeister going crazy trying to make sure every single piece of food coming off the grill is properly cooked. For that reason, main-course proteins like ribs, chops, steaks, and chicken parts should be completely precooked at home (they can even be cooked the day before and refrigerated), then brought to the picnic for a warm-up over the fire and a final slathering of barbecue sauce. *A note to the organizer:* In addition to paper plates and utensils, also remember to bring a big roll of heavy-duty foil. Items like chicken legs, brisket, and ribs need to be cooked covered on the grill, and public grills don't usually have lids; you'll need the foil to perform that task.

Mayo Gets a Bum Rap

Concerned about taking salads or sandwiches made with mayonnaise on a picnic because the mayonnaise might spoil? You're blaming the wrong ingredient: Mayo has a clean record. The rumors began decades ago with *homemade* mayonnaise, which contains raw eggs; commercial brands, made with pasteurized eggs, have a high acid content (they contain vinegar and lemon juice) that actually *prevents* the growth of food-poisoning bacteria. The real culprits? Low-acid salad ingredients and sandwich fillings, such as tuna, ham, chicken, eggs, potatoes, and macaroni. When mishandled (left unrefrigerated too long, or prepared with hands or utensils that have not been washed properly), they can encourage bacterial growth.

KEEP IT COLD (AND SAFE)

When it comes to picnics and tailgates, keeping your food cold is a matter of personal safety as well as enjoyment. Here are some tips for ensuring that your food stays chilly when the weather is hot.

- **THE COLDER THE FOOD IS BEFORE YOU PUT IT IN THE COOLER, THE LONGER YOUR SPREAD WILL STAY FRESH.** Refrigerate picnic items the night before and don't pack the cooler until right before leaving.

- **PICK UP AN EXTRA BAG OF ICE AND USE IT TO CHILL THE COOLER BEFORE PACKING IT.** Close the lid and let it chill for at least forty-five minutes. If the ice turns slushy by the time you start packing, toss it out and add fresh cubes. This is worth doing even if you use freezer packs—the packs will work better because they're going into a cold cooler. Also, if you will be transporting anything in a thermos (like our cold Honeydew and Lime Soup on page 93), chill the container in advance, either setting it in the freezer for an hour or filling it with ice water for fifteen minutes.

- **CONSIDER TAKING TWO COOLERS: ONE FOR FOOD, ONE FOR DRINKS.** That way, perishables won't be exposed to warm air every time someone grabs a soda. If you can tote only one cooler, pack dessert (which you'll eat last) at the bottom and the snacks you want right away (dips, cheeses, etc.) on top.

- **A FULL COOLER KEEPS FOOD COLD LONGER THAN A PARTIALLY EMPTY ONE.** Pack the top (cold air travels down) and any empty spots with ice, frozen juice boxes or water bottles, or freezer packs, or simply fill in the space with terry towels—they not only retain the cold air but they also keep the hot air out.

- **USE FREEZER PACKS EFFICIENTLY.** Line the cooler with them, top, bottom, and sides, and tuck some in the middle.

- **AT THE PICNIC SITE, KEEP THE COOLER CLOSED AND IN THE SHADE.**

- **IN GENERAL, DON'T LEAVE FOOD OUT LONGER THAN AN HOUR.**

The Tailgate Potluck

Tailgating requires the same sort of attention to planning and food safety that picnicking does, but here are some additional considerations to keep in mind.

- If you'll be transporting hot food in an insulated serving carafe (like soup or a warm drink), heat up the container first: Fill it with boiling water and let it sit for ten minutes, then dump it out before refilling it.

- If the menu includes grilling, ask whoever brings the grill to function as host, with everyone meeting up at that car. To make finding the car easier, put out a welcome mat by flying helium balloons of a particular color or hoisting a pennant flag.

- Make sure any raw food (chicken, burgers, fish) is double-wrapped or -bagged to prevent any cross-contaminating spillage in the cooler.

- Plan to arrive at least three hours before the sporting event if you're going to be cooking to allow plenty of time for set-up, food prep, the leisurely partaking of your potluck, and clean-up. Tailgating is no fun if you have to wolf your food down.

- Be prepared for the weather. If it's going to be cold, dress in layers and bring a couple of extra sweaters or jackets just in case. Have a bottle of sunblock in the car; even if there is a chill in the air, if it's a sunny day you can end up with sunburn. And always plan for rain; keep your gear in the car and, if you think you might tailgate often, consider getting a portable canopy.

- In addition to their potluck dish, ask everyone to bring their own chairs.

- If you're using a charcoal grill, bring a large disposable aluminum pan (or several) with you. Dump the used coals in the pan and douse them well with water (bring a couple of gallons with you) before bagging them up and putting them in the garbage.

Like picnicking, your tailgate can be as involved, casual, even elegant as you want it to be, which is part of the fun. Internet tailgate supply sites are a great source of ideas, from grills and coolers to tents and tables to flagpoles and fun stuff like magnetic and suction-cup cozies that will keep your drink from sliding off the hood of your car.

· Mother's Day
BRUNCH

MENU

Fizzy Cranberry-
Lemonade Punch

Citrus Salad with
Sherry Dressing

Mini Crab Cakes with
Lemon Sauce

Broccoli and Cheddar Crepes

Syrupy Banana-Nut
Overnight French Toast

Crustless Leek and
Gruyère Quiche

Chocolate Nemesis

Sorbet Terrine with
Plum Compote

For Mom's day we've made this brunch menu a bit elegant—and a bit indulgent. Instead of offering mimosas, the classic brunch cocktail, we're serving a sprightly cranberry-lemonade punch that can be enjoyed with or without alcohol. Mini crab cakes start the festivities off right. They are followed by a generous buffet of brunch favorites—crepes, French toast, and quiche—as well as a refreshing fruit salad to balance the richness of the other dishes. If you like, add a plate of bacon or breakfast sausages. Finally, Mom gets to pick between two luscious desserts—a deep, dark chocolate cake or an eye-catching sorbet terrine—or enjoy them both! After all, it's her day.

FIZZY CRANBERRY-LEMONADE PUNCH

TOTAL TIME 15 minutes · **MAKES** 9 cups or 12 servings

This punch is wonderfully versatile. It's a satisfying quencher as is, but you can also have vodka and dark rum available for grown-up guests to spike their glasses, if they like.

1 In large pitcher, stir cranberry-juice cocktail and lemonade concentrate until blended.

2 Stir in seltzer and ice cubes, if you like. Add orange slices and serve.

4 cups cranberry-juice cocktail, chilled

1 container (6 ounces) frozen lemonade concentrate, thawed

1 bottle (1 liter) plain seltzer or club soda, chilled

ice cubes (optional)

1 small orange, cut into ¼-inch-thick slices and each slice cut in half

EACH SERVING
About 81 calories, 0g protein, 21g carbohydrate, 0g fat, 0g fiber, 0mg cholesterol, 23mg sodium

POTLUCK PREP Prepare the punch through step 1 and transport in a covered container, along with a liter of seltzer and the orange slices, stored in a zip-tight plastic bag. Transfer the punch to a pitcher at the potluck, add seltzer, ice cubes, if using, and orange slices, and start serving.

CITRUS SALAD WITH SHERRY DRESSING

TOTAL TIME 30 minutes · MAKES 12 side-dish servings

A splash of sherry gives this refreshing fruit salad an added layer of complexity.

1 Prepare dressing: In large bowl, with wire whisk, mix sherry, vinegar, mustard, salt, and pepper. In thin, steady stream, whisk in oil until blended.

2 Add apple slices to dressing in bowl and toss to coat. Cut peel and white pith from oranges and grapefruit. Holding oranges and grapefruit over small bowl to catch juice, cut out sections from between membranes. (If you like, squeeze juice from membranes and reserve for another use.) Add orange and grapefruit sections to dressing in bowl; toss to coat.

3 Arrange watercress on platter. Spoon fruit mixture and dressing over watercress.

Sherry Dressing

¼ cup dry sherry

2 tablespoons red wine vinegar

2 teaspoons Dijon mustard

½ teaspoon salt

¼ teaspoon coarsely ground black pepper

¼ cup olive oil

Citrus Salad

2 large Granny Smith apples, cored and cut into paper-thin slices

4 large navel oranges

2 large pink grapefruit

2 bunches watercress (4 ounces each), tough stems trimmed

EACH SERVING
About 109 calories, 2g protein, 16g carbohydrate, 5g total fat (1g saturated), 3g fiber, 0mg cholesterol, 127mg sodium

POTLUCK PREP Transport apples, oranges, and grapefruit tossed with the dressing in an airtight container or zip-tight plastic bag, and the washed and trimmed watercress in another plastic bag. Bring serving platter and tongs. Right before serving, arrange watercress on platter and spoon fruit and dressing over it.

MINI CRAB CAKES WITH LEMON SAUCE

ACTIVE TIME 25 minutes · **TOTAL TIME** 40 minutes plus chilling
MAKES 50 mini crab cakes

Mom is going to love these tasty little mouthfuls. The beauty is they can be prepared completely ahead of time then put in the oven briefly to reheat. Be sure to arrive in plenty of time to get them reheated before the other guests start coming!

1 In 10-inch skillet, melt butter over medium heat. Add onion, red pepper, and celery. Cook until vegetables are tender, about 10 minutes, stirring frequently. Let cool.

2 In large bowl, stir vegetables, mayonnaise, sour cream, mustard, lemon peel, salt, and ground red pepper until blended; stir in crabmeat and bread crumbs just until mixed. Cover and refrigerate 30 minutes.

3 Meanwhile, prepare sauce: In small bowl, stir together mayonnaise, sour cream, lemon peel and juice, salt, and ground red pepper until blended. Makes about 1/2 cup. Cover and refrigerate until ready to serve.

4 Preheat oven to 400°F. Lightly grease 2 cookie sheets. Drop level tablespoons of chilled crab mixture, pressing lightly, onto prepared cookie sheets. Bake until golden brown, about 15 minutes.

2 tablespoons butter or margarine

1 small onion, finely chopped

1/2 red pepper, finely chopped

1 stalk celery, finely chopped

1/4 cup light mayonnaise

1 tablespoon sour cream

2 teaspoons grainy Dijon mustard

1/2 teaspoon freshly grated lemon peel

1/4 teaspoon salt

1/8 teaspoon ground red pepper (cayenne)

1 pound lump crabmeat, picked over

1 cup fresh bread crumbs (about 2 slices bread)

Lemon Sauce

1/4 cup light mayonnaise

1/4 cup sour cream

1 teaspoon freshly grated lemon peel

1 tablespoon fresh lemon juice

pinch salt

pinch ground red pepper (cayenne)

5 Top each crab cake with about ½ teaspoon lemon sauce. Serve hot.

EACH CRAB CAKE WITH SAUCE
About 28 calories, 2g protein, 1g carbohydrate, 2g total fat (1g saturated), 0g fiber, 12mg cholesterol, 71mg sodium

POTLUCK PREP You can prepare these up to several hours ahead and refrigerate after baking. Transport them on their baking sheets, covered with plastic wrap, with the lemon sauce in a small airtight container; bring a serving platter. Have your host preheat the oven for you and pop them in to heat through again, about 10 minutes. Transfer the crab cakes to the platter, top each with a little dollop of lemon sauce, and set out for guests.

BROCCOLI AND CHEDDAR CREPES

ACTIVE TIME 45 minutes · **TOTAL TIME** 1 hour plus chilling
MAKES 12 crepes

Don't let the idea of making crepes from scratch put you off preparing this dish. Crepes are very simple to cook and, even better, they can be made ahead and reheated when you need them.

3 large eggs

2/3 cup all-purpose flour

3 cups reduced-fat (2%) milk

4 tablespoons butter or margarine, melted

3/4 teaspoon salt

1 small red onion, sliced

2 tablespoons cornstarch

2 packages (10 ounces each) frozen chopped broccoli, thawed

1/4 teaspoon coarsely ground black pepper

1 package (8 ounces) shredded sharp Cheddar cheese (2 cups)

1/4 cup loosely packed fresh parsley leaves, chopped

1   In blender, combine eggs, flour, 1½ cups milk, 2 tablespoons butter, and ½ teaspoon salt. Cover and blend until smooth, scraping down sides of blender occasionally. Transfer batter to medium bowl; cover and refrigerate at least 1 hour or overnight to allow flour to absorb liquid.

2   Lightly brush 10-inch nonstick skillet with some melted butter and heat over medium heat 1 minute. With wire whisk, thoroughly mix batter to blend well. Pour scant ¼ cup batter into skillet; tilt pan to coat bottom completely with batter. Cook crepe until top is dry and set and underside is lightly browned, about 2 minutes. With spatula, loosen edge of crepe; turn over. Cook until second side is browned, 30 seconds to 1 minute.

3   Slip crepe onto waxed paper. Repeat with remaining batter, brushing pan lightly with butter before cooking each crepe and stacking crepes between layers of waxed paper. You should have at least 12 crepes. The crepes will keep, tightly wrapped in plastic, in refrigerator up to 2 days.

4 Meanwhile, preheat oven to 400°F.

5 In 12-inch nonstick skillet, heat remaining tablespoon butter over medium heat until hot. Add onion and cook until tender and beginning to brown, 6 to 8 minutes, stirring occasionally. In cup, stir together cornstarch and remaining 1½ cups milk. To onion in skillet, add milk mixture, broccoli, remaining ¼ teaspoon salt, and pepper. Heat to boiling; boil 1 minute. Remove skillet from heat; stir in 1½ cups Cheddar.

6 Place crepes on surface; spread generous ¼ cup broccoli mixture on half of each crepe. Starting from side with broccoli, roll up crepes and place, seam side down, in shallow 2-quart glass or ceramic baking dish. Sprinkle with remaining ½ cup Cheddar.

7 Bake until cheese melts and crepes are heated through, about 15 minutes. Sprinkle with parsley.

EACH CREPE
About 210, 10g protein, 13g carbohydrate, 12g total fat (6g saturated), 2g fiber, 78mg cholesterol, 362mg sodium

POTLUCK PREP Depending on your host's preference, you can either assemble the dish right before arriving and heat it through at the potluck before serving or bake it at home and transport it to the potluck in an insulated food carrier. Either way, bring the parsley in a small zip-tight plastic bag and garnish the crepes right before serving.

SYRUPY BANANA-NUT OVERNIGHT FRENCH TOAST

ACTIVE TIME **20 minutes** · TOTAL TIME **65 minutes plus chilling and standing**
MAKES **8 main-dish servings**

This is the perfect dish for the host to assign to herself. Put it together the night before, then pop it into the oven before guests start arriving.

1 In microwave-safe small bowl, heat butter in microwave oven on High 1 minute or until melted. Stir brown sugar into butter until moistened. With fingertips, press sugar mixture over bottom of 13" by 9" baking dish. (It's fine if mixture does not cover bottom.) Spread fresh or dried fruit over sugar mixture; top with bread slices.

2 In large bowl, with wire whisk, beat eggs; whisk in milk, vanilla, and cinnamon. Slowly pour milk mixture over bread; press bread down to absorb egg mixture. Sprinkle with nuts. Cover with plastic wrap and refrigerate at least 2 hours or overnight.

3 Preheat oven to 350°F. Remove plastic wrap from baking dish. Bake until bread is golden brown and knife inserted in center comes out clean, 45 to 50 minutes. Let stand 10 minutes before serving.

6 tablespoons butter or margarine

1½ cups packed brown sugar

5 large ripe bananas, cut diagonally into ½-inch-thick slices; or 3 to 4 very ripe pears or peaches (about 1½ pounds), sliced; or 1 cup dried cherries, cranberries, or raisins

1 long loaf (12 ounces) French or Italian bread, cut crosswise into 1-inch-thick slices

6 large eggs

2 cups milk

2 teaspoons vanilla extract

1 teaspoon ground cinnamon

½ cup sliced almonds or coarsely chopped walnuts or pecans

EACH SERVING
About 570 calories, 13g protein, 89g carbohydrate, 20g total fat (11g saturated), 5g fiber, 191mg cholesterol, 465mg sodium

POTLUCK PREP **Bake right before leaving. Cover with foil and transport in an insulated food carrier. Don't allow baking dish to stand before putting it in the carrier; it will lose too much heat.**

CRUSTLESS LEEK AND GRUYÈRE QUICHE

ACTIVE TIME 20 minutes · **TOTAL TIME** 50 minutes · **MAKES** 8 main-dish servings

A quiche without a crust? Don't worry—the delicate custard is so smooth and tasty, you'll never miss the pastry.

1   Preheat oven to 350°F. Grease 10-inch quiche dish or 9½-inch deep-dish pie plate.

2   Cut off roots and trim dark green tops from leeks. Discard any tough outer leaves. Cut each leek lengthwise in half, then crosswise into ¼-inch-thick slices. Rinse leeks thoroughly in large bowl of cold water, swishing to remove sand. With hands, transfer leeks to colander to drain, leaving sand in bottom of bowl. Repeat process, changing water several times, until all sand is removed. Shake colander several times to remove excess water from leeks.

3   In 12-inch nonstick skillet, heat oil over medium heat 1 minute. Add leeks and ¼ teaspoon salt; cook until leeks are tender and browned, 12 to 14 minutes, stirring frequently. Transfer leeks to prepared quiche dish and spread evenly.

4   Meanwhile, in bowl, with wire whisk, beat eggs, milk, cornstarch, remaining ¼ teaspoon salt, and pepper until well

1 pound leeks (about 3 medium)

1 tablespoon olive oil

½ teaspoon salt

6 large eggs

2½ cups whole milk

1 tablespoon cornstarch

¼ teaspoon coarsely ground black pepper

4 ounces Gruyère cheese, shredded (1 cup)

blended. Pour egg mixture over leeks in dish. Sprinkle with Gruyère.

5 Bake quiche until knife inserted in center comes out clean, 30 to 35 minutes. Cool on wire rack for 5 minutes.

EACH SERVING
About 195 calories, 12g protein, 8g carbohydrate, 13g total fat (6g saturated), 1g fiber, 185mg cholesterol, 280mg sodium

POTLUCK PREP Bake right before leaving. Remove from oven; cover tightly with foil. Transport in an insulated food carrier.

CHOCOLATE NEMESIS

ACTIVE TIME 35 minutes · **TOTAL TIME** 65 minutes plus cooling and chilling
MAKES 16 servings

This cake is chocolate heaven.

1   Preheat oven to 325°F. Grease bottom and side of 9-inch springform pan. Line bottom of pan with parchment paper. Dust sides of pan with flour. Set pan on wide sheet of heavy-duty foil and tightly wrap foil up outside of pan to prevent water from seeping in during baking.

2   In 4-quart saucepan, heat water and ½ cup sugar over medium-high heat until sugar completely dissolves, stirring occasionally. Add chocolate and butter to mixture in saucepan; stir constantly until melted. Remove pan from heat; cool chocolate mixture slightly, about 30 minutes.

3   Meanwhile, in large bowl, with mixer on high speed, beat eggs with remaining ½ cup sugar until mixture thickens and triples in volume, 6 to 8 minutes. With rubber spatula, fold warm chocolate mixture into egg mixture until completely blended.

4   Pour batter into prepared springform pan; place in large (17" by 11½") roasting pan and set on oven rack. Pour enough *boiling*

½ cup water

1 cup sugar

1 pound good-quality bittersweet chocolate, chopped

1 cup unsalted butter (2 sticks), cut up

7 large eggs, at room temperature

softly whipped cream or crème fraîche

fresh raspberries for garnish

water into roasting pan to come halfway up side of springform pan.

5 Bake cake until edge begins to set and a thin crust forms on top, 30 to 35 minutes. Carefully remove springform pan from water bath and place on wire rack. Cool cake to room temperature. Cover and refrigerate overnight.

6 About 30 minutes before serving, run sharp knife around edge of pan to loosen cake; remove foil and side of pan. Invert cake onto waxed paper; peel off parchment. Turn cake right side up onto platter. Serve with whipped cream and berries.

EACH SERVING
About 345 calories, 5g protein, 22g carbohydrate, 27g total fat (15g saturated fat), 1g fiber, 125mg cholesterol, 45mg sodium

POTLUCK PREP Prepare cake the day before; transport in its springform pan, along with a serving plate, the berries, and whipped cream or crème fraîche in an airtight container. At potluck, remove cake as instructed in step 6, cut into slices, and, right before serving, set out berries and whipped cream so guests can serve themselves.

SORBET TERRINE WITH PLUM COMPOTE

TOTAL TIME 35 minutes plus freezing · **MAKES** 12 servings

The icy fruit flavors of this beautiful frozen dessert are a delicious foil to the indulgent richness of Chocolate Nemesis (page 30).

1 Prepare terrine: Remove mango sorbet from freezer; let stand 10 minutes to soften slightly.

2 Meanwhile, line 8½" by 4¼" metal loaf pan with plastic wrap, letting wrap extend over sides and ends. Spread mango sorbet in prepared pan in an even layer. Sprinkle with half of cookie crumbs. Freeze until sorbet is firm, about 30 minutes.

3 Repeat with softened ice cream and remaining cookie crumbs; return pan to freezer for about 30 minutes.

4 Top with softened raspberry sorbet, then wrap terrine with plastic wrap; freeze overnight.

5. Meanwhile, prepare compote: In food processor with knife blade attached, pulse plums until chopped. In 3-quart saucepan,

Sorbet Terrine
1 pint mango sorbet

2/3 cup amaretti cookie crumbs

1 pint chocolate-chip ice cream

1 pint raspberry sorbet

EACH SERVING TERRINE
About 170 calories, 2g protein, 32g carbohydrate, 4g total fat (2g saturated), 1g fiber, 8mg cholesterol, 20mg sodium

POTLUCK PREP To avoid any disastrous melting, this recipe should be prepared by the host or assigned to a guest who lives within ten minutes of the potluck. Prepare terrine and compote several days before. Transport terrine in loaf pan set in ice in a cooler and the compote in an airtight container; bring serving platter and small serving dish for compote. Keep terrine in freezer until serving time. Right before serving, unmold and slice as directed in step 6.

combine plums and sugar; heat to boiling over high heat, stirring. Reduce heat to medium-low and simmer until plums soften and sauce thickens, about 20 minutes, stirring often. Stir in lemon juice. Cover and refrigerate at least 2 hours or up to 1 week. Makes about 1¾ cups.

6 To serve, unwrap terrine and invert onto platter; discard plastic. With knife run under hot water, slice terrine. Serve with compote.

Plum Compote
1½ pounds ripe plums
(about 6), pitted and cut
into wedges

¼ cup sugar

1 tablespoon fresh lemon juice

EACH TABLESPOON COMPOTE
About 20 calories, 0g protein,
5g carbohydrate, 0g fat, 0g fiber,
0mg cholesterol, 0mg sodium

· Potluck ·
PATIO PARTY

—— MENU ——

Simple Sangria

Chicken and Beef Saté

Three-Bean and
Corn Salad

Shrimp with Asian
Barbecue Sauce

Spiced Kielbasa and
Summer Fruit Kabobs

Scallop and
Cherry Tomato Skewers

Grasshopper Cake

Make your inaugural barbecue a potluck! Kabobs are the theme here. Ask your guests to bring their contributions already skewered and grill ready, with the basting or dipping sauce in a small container. The shrimp skewers are served over a bed of romaine; for your other kabob offerings, prepare a large platter of rice (basmati or jasmine rice would be a nice choice) and serve the kabobs mounded around it (minus the skewers) so your diners can take what they like. Our Three-Bean and Corn Salad rounds out the meal. The fruit-filled sangria announces that summer is here, and Grasshopper Cake, a delicious combination of mint and chocolate, ends the meal on a refreshing note.

SIMPLE SANGRIA

TOTAL TIME 10 minutes plus chilling · **MAKES** 12 servings

Be sure to ladle a piece of fruit or two into each cup as you serve it.

1 In 3- to 4-quart pitcher, combine wine, orange juice, brandy, and sugar; stir until sugar dissolves.

2 Stir in fruit and cucumber. Cover and refrigerate until well chilled, at least 3 hours or overnight.

3 To serve, stir seltzer into pitcher. Fill glasses with ice and pour sangria.

1 bottle (1½ liters) red wine

1½ cups fresh orange juice

⅓ cup brandy

⅓ cup sugar

2 nectarines, pitted and cut into wedges

1 orange, cut in half, then sliced

1 lemon, sliced

1 Kirby (pickling) cucumber, sliced

3 cups seltzer or club soda, chilled

ice cubes

EACH SERVING
About 160 calories, 1g protein, 16g carbohydrate, 0g fat, 1g fiber, 0mg cholesterol, 20mg sodium

POTLUCK PREP Prepare the recipe through step 2 in advance enough to allow proper chilling. Transport in a covered pitcher, along with a liter bottle of seltzer. Add seltzer right before serving.

CHICKEN AND BEEF SATÉ

ACTIVE TIME 45 minutes · **TOTAL TIME** 1 hour plus marinating
MAKES 6 main-dish servings

Saté is the perfect appetizer for a kabob-themed get-together. The thinly sliced chicken and beef get nice and charry over the fire, and the accompanying relish and peanut sauce provide even more flavor.

1 Prepare saté: slice chicken cutlets lengthwise into ¾-inch-wide strips; place in medium bowl.

2 Holding knife almost parallel to cutting surface, slice steak crosswise into thin strips; place in another bowl.

3 From limes, grate 2 teaspoons peel and squeeze 2 tablespoons juice.

4 In small bowl, with fork, mix lime peel and juice, soy sauce, ginger, sugar, and garlic. Stir half of soy-sauce mixture into chicken. Stir remaining soy-sauce mixture into beef. Cover and refrigerate both bowls 30 minutes to marinate.

Saté

1 pound chicken-breast cutlets

1 (1-inch-thick) boneless beef top sirloin steak (about 1¼ pounds)

2 large limes

¼ cup soy sauce

1 tablespoon grated, peeled fresh ginger

2 teaspoons sugar

2 garlic cloves, crushed with garlic press

24 (10-inch) wooden skewers

EACH SERVING
About 250 calories, 40g protein, 2g carbohydrate, 8g total fat (3g saturated), 0g fiber, 103mg cholesterol, 435mg sodium

POTLUCK PREP Transport threaded skewers, ready for the grill, in a cooler in zip-tight plastic bags, one for the chicken skewers, one for the beef skewers. (You might want to double bag them to prevent any leaks.) Transport relish and peanut sauce in separate airtight containers. Also bring a serving platter that will accommodate cooked skewers, plus serving bowls for relish and sauce.

5 Soak wooden skewers in water 20 minutes. Meanwhile, prepare Cucumber Relish: In medium bowl, with spoon, mix cucumbers, vinegar, onion, oil, and crushed red pepper. Makes about 2½ cups.

6 Prepare peanut sauce: In medium bowl, with wire whisk, mix peanut butter, hot water, vinegar, soy sauce, molasses, and crushed red pepper until smooth. Makes about ⅔ cup.

7 Thread chicken strips and beef strips separately on wooden skewers, accordion-style.

8 Prepare outdoor grill for direct grilling over medium heat.

9 Place skewers on hot grill rack and grill until just cooked through, 3 to 7 minutes, turning once.

10 Serve skewers with Spicy Peanut Sauce and Cucumber Relish.

Cucumber Relish

4 medium Kirby (pickling) cucumbers (4 ounces each), diced

¼ cup seasoned rice vinegar

2 tablespoons diced red onion

1 tablespoon vegetable oil

¼ teaspoon crushed red pepper

EACH ¼ CUP RELISH
About 30 calories, 0g protein, 4g carbohydrate, 1g total fat (0g saturated), 0g fiber, 0mg cholesterol, 160mg sodium

Spicy Peanut Sauce

¼ cup creamy peanut butter

¼ cup very hot water

4 teaspoons seasoned rice vinegar

1 tablespoon soy sauce

1 tablespoon light (mild) molasses

⅛ teaspoon crushed red pepper

EACH TABLESPOON SAUCE
About 45 calories, 2g protein, 3g carbohydrate, 3g total fat (1g saturated), 0.5g fiber, 0mg cholesterol, 170mg sodium

THREE-BEAN AND CORN SALAD

TOTAL TIME 35 minutes plus chilling · **MAKES** 7 cups or 12 side-dish servings

This is a tasty twist on bean salad, adding tender-crisp green beans and summer-fresh corn, tossed with a vibrant dressing of lime juice, Dijon, honey, and tarragon.

1 In 2-quart saucepan, heat *1 inch water* with 1 teaspoon salt to boiling over high heat. Add green beans; heat to boiling. Reduce heat to medium-low; simmer until beans are tender-crisp, about 5 minutes.

2 While green beans are cooking, prepare dressing: In small bowl, with wire whisk, mix shallot, oil, lime juice, vinegar, honey, tarragon, mustard, remaining ¾ teaspoon salt, and black pepper until blended.

3 Drain green beans. Rinse with cold running water to stop cooking; drain again. Transfer beans to large serving bowl. Add canned beans, corn, and red pepper to bowl.

4 Add dressing to bean mixture; toss until evenly coated. Cover and refrigerate at least 1 hour to blend flavors or up to 8 hours.

1¾ teaspoons salt

12 ounces green and/or wax beans, trimmed and cut into 1-inch pieces

1 small shallot, finely chopped

¼ cup olive oil

3 tablespoons fresh lime juice (from 2 limes)

2 tablespoons white wine vinegar

2 tablespoons honey

1 tablespoon chopped fresh tarragon leaves

1 tablespoon Dijon mustard

¼ teaspoon black pepper

1 can (15 to 19 ounces) red kidney beans, rinsed and drained

1 can (15 to 19 ounces) cannellini beans, rinsed and drained

1⅓ cups fresh corn kernels (from 3 to 4 ears)

1 medium red pepper, cut into ½-inch pieces

EACH SERVING
About 160 calories, 5g protein, 24g carbohydrate, 5g total fat (1g saturated), 6g fiber, 0mg cholesterol, 315mg sodium

POTLUCK PREP Prepare in advance for proper chilling. Transport in a covered serving bowl.

SHRIMP WITH ASIAN BARBECUE SAUCE

TOTAL TIME 20 minutes · **MAKES** 4 main-dish servings

Hoisin sauce is tasty on its own, but here its flavor is enhanced with the addition of fresh ginger and five-spice powder. If using wooden or bamboo skewers, soak them in water at least 20 minutes first.

1 In small bowl, stir hoisin sauce, ketchup, ginger, five-spice powder, and 1 tablespoon vinegar to make barbecue sauce. Remove ¼ cup barbecue sauce to ramekin; stir in water and remaining 1 tablespoon vinegar and reserve to use as dipping sauce.

2 Thread shrimp tightly on skewers. Brush shrimp with some barbecue sauce from bowl.

3 Lightly grease grill rack. Prepare outdoor grill for direct grilling over medium heat.

4 Place shrimp on hot grill rack and cook 2 minutes. Brush with some barbecue sauce; turn and brush with remaining sauce from bowl and grill until shrimp turn opaque throughout, 1 to 2 minutes longer.

5 Arrange romaine on platter. Serve shrimp on skewers over romaine with reserved dipping sauce.

⅓ cup hoisin sauce

3 tablespoons ketchup

1½ teaspoons grated, peeled fresh ginger

¼ teaspoon Chinese five-spice powder

2 tablespoons rice vinegar

2 tablespoons water

1¼ pounds large shrimp, shelled and deveined with tail part of shell left on if you like

4 (10- to 12-inch) skewers

romaine lettuce leaves

EACH SERVING
About 185 calories, 25g protein, 13g carbohydrate, 3g total fat (1g saturated), 1g fiber, 175mg cholesterol, 540mg sodium

POTLUCK PREP Transport threaded skewers, ready for the grill, in a cooler in a zip-tight plastic bag (you might want to double bag to prevent any leaking) and the two sauces in airtight containers. Separate the romaine into leaves, wash, pat dry, and place in a plastic bag. Also bring a serving platter and small serving bowl for the dipping sauce.

SPICED KIELBASA AND SUMMER FRUIT KABOBS

ACTIVE TIME 10 minutes · **TOTAL TIME** 16 minutes
MAKES 4 to 6 main-dish servings

If you haven't tried fruit on the grill, you're in for a treat. The heat of the fire caramelizes the natural sugars in the apricots and plums, making them a perfect partner for the rich smoky taste of the sausage.

1 Alternately thread kielbasa, apricots, and plums onto skewers. In cup, combine marmalade and five-spice powder.

2 Prepare outdoor grill for covered direct grilling over medium heat.

3 Place skewers on hot grill rack. Cover grill and cook until kielbasa browns and fruit chars slightly, about 5 minutes, turning skewers occasionally. Uncover grill. Brush marmalade mixture all over kielbasa and fruit. Cook 1 to 2 minutes longer, turning occasionally.

1 package (16 ounces) light kielbasa or other smoked sausage, cut into 1-inch chunks

3 apricots, pitted and cut into quarters

2 ripe plums or peaches, pitted and cut into 1-inch chunks

4 to 6 (10-inch) metal skewers

3 tablespoons sweet orange marmalade

1 tablespoon Chinese five-spice powder

EACH SERVING
About 340 calories, 17g protein, 22g carbohydrate, 22g fat (8g saturated), 2g fiber, 76mg cholesterol, 1,032mg sodium

POTLUCK PREP Transport threaded skewers, ready for the grill, in a cooler in a zip-tight plastic bag and the marmalade glaze in a small airtight container.

SCALLOP AND CHERRY TOMATO SKEWERS

TOTAL TIME 25 minutes · **MAKES** 4 main-dish servings

Keep a close eye on the scallops as they cook. Remove from grill as soon as they're opaque all the way through or they'll become rubbery.

1 Soak skewers in hot water at least 20 minutes.

2 Meanwhile, from lemon, grate 1½ teaspoons peel and squeeze 1 tablespoon juice. In small bowl, whisk lemon peel and juice, oil, mustard, and salt until blended; set aside.

3 Thread 3 tomatoes and 2 scallops alternately on each skewer, beginning and ending with tomatoes.

4 Prepare outdoor grill for direct grilling over medium heat.

5 Brush scallops and tomatoes with half of mustard mixture; place on hot grill rack. Cook 7 to 9 minutes, turning several times. Brush with remaining mustard mixture and cook until scallops just turn opaque throughout, about 5 minutes longer.

8 (8-inch) wooden skewers

1 lemon

2 tablespoons olive oil

2 tablespoons Dijon mustard

⅛ teaspoon salt

24 cherry tomatoes

16 large sea scallops (1¼ pounds)

EACH SERVING
About 215 calories, 25g protein, 9g carbohydrate, 9g total fat (1g saturated), 1g fiber, 47mg cholesterol, 355mg sodium

POTLUCK PREP Transport threaded skewers, ready for the grill, in a cooler in a zip-tight plastic bag and the mustard glaze in a small airtight container.

GRASSHOPPER CAKE

ACTIVE TIME 50 minutes · **TOTAL TIME** 65 minutes plus cooling · **MAKES** 12 servings

This icebox cake will have guests clamoring for the recipe. Cold from the refrigerator, it will cool and refresh with its light whipped cream filling spiked with the unexpected addition of mint.

1 Quot;Preheat oven to 350°F. Grease 15½" by 10½" jelly-roll pan; line with waxed paper. On another sheet of waxed paper, combine flour, cocoa, and salt.

2 Quot;In large bowl, with mixer on low speed, beat butter and 1¼ cups sugar just until blended. Increase speed to high; beat until mixture is light and creamy, about 3 minutes, frequently scraping down bowl with rubber spatula. Reduce speed to low; add eggs, 1 at a time, beating well after each addition. Add flour mixture; beat just until combined, occasionally scraping bowl.

3 Quot;Pour batter into prepared pan and spread evenly. Bake until toothpick inserted in center comes out clean, 15 to 18 minutes. Cool cake completely in pan on wire rack, about 40 minutes.

4 Quot;Meanwhile, with vegetable peeler, shave a long side of each thin mint lengthwise to equal ½ cup curls. (You can only shave

1 cup all-purpose flour

½ cup unsweetened cocoa

¼ teaspoon salt

½ cup butter or margarine (1 stick), softened

1¼ cups plus 1 tablespoon sugar

3 large eggs

20 crème de menthe thin mints (from 4.67-ounce package)

1½ cups heavy or whipping cream

about half of each mint before it breaks.)
Reserve curls for sprinkling on top of
assembled cake. Chop broken pieces
and set aside for use in filling (you will
have about ⅓ cup chopped mints).

5 With small knife, loosen cake sides from
waxed paper; invert cake onto cutting board.
Carefully remove waxed paper.
With sharp knife, trim ¼ inch
from each side of cake. Cut cake
crosswise into 3 equal rectangles
(about 9½" by 4½" each).

6 In medium bowl, with mixer
on medium speed, beat cream
and remaining 1 tablespoon sugar
until stiff peaks form. With rubber
spatula, gently fold chopped mints
into whipped cream.

7 Place 1 cake rectangle on
serving plate; top with 1 generous
cup whipped-cream mixture and
spread evenly. Repeat 2 times
with remaining cake and cream
mixture. Sprinkle top with reserved mint
curls. Cover and refrigerate cake if not
serving right away.

EACH SERVING
About 360 calories, 4g protein,
36g carbohydrate, 24g total fat
(15g saturated), 1g fiber, 116mg
cholesterol, 165mg sodium

POTLUCK PREP Transport cake in cake carrier. If traveling any distance, carry in a
cooler. Keep refrigerated until time to serve.

Family Reunion
PICNIC

— MENU —

Tortilla Spirals

Stuffed Eggs

Black Bean Dip

Campfire Corn with
Herb Butter

Sweet and Tangy
Barbecue Chicken

Brisket with Chunky
Barbecue Sauce

Ribs Supreme

Creamy
Cucumber-Dill Salad

Antipasto Salad

Chunky Greek Salad

S'more Bars

Peanut Butter and
Jelly Bars

This picnic in the park pulls out all the stops for a gala gathering of the extended family. To feed your crowd, we offer a diverse selection of appetizers to quell any hunger pains while the grills are getting fired up, as well as a yummy choice of side salads. S'mores Bars and PB&J Bars offer a sweet finish for kids and grown-ups alike. For tips on planning, see When Your Potluck is a Picnic, page 12.

TORTILLA SPIRALS

TOTAL TIME 35 minutes plus chilling · **MAKES** 144 spirals

You get two for one with this recipe—two different fillings for two flavors of spirals—smoked salmon and dried tomato.

1 Prepare Smoked Salmon Filling: In medium bowl, with spoon, mix cream cheese, smoked salmon, capers, and dill until blended.

2 Prepare Dried Tomato Filling: In medium bowl, combine cream cheese, dried tomatoes, spreadable cheese, and basil until blended.

3 Spread each of the fillings evenly over 4 tortillas (4 with salmon, 4 with tomato). Roll each tortilla up tightly, jelly-roll fashion. Wrap each roll in plastic wrap and refrigerate until firm enough to slice, at least 4 hours or overnight.

4 To serve, unwrap plastic around tortilla rolls and trim ends. Cut rolls into slightly less than ½-inch-thick slices.

Smoked Salmon Filling
1½ packages (8 ounces each) cream cheese, softened

4 ounces thinly sliced smoked salmon, chopped

3 tablespoons capers, drained and chopped

¼ cup loosely packed fresh dill, chopped

Dried Tomato Filling
1 package (8 ounces) cream cheese, softened

10 dried tomato halves, packed in herb-seasoned olive oil, drained and chopped

1 container (5.2 ounces) spreadable cheese with pepper

⅓ cup packed fresh basil leaves, chopped

8 (10-inch) flour tortillas

POTLUCK PREP Prepare far enough in advance to allow time for proper chilling. You can either slice spirals at home and arrange them in a large rectangular glass dish, separating each layer with waxed paper, then transfer them to serving plates at the picnic, or transport the wrapped tortillas to the picnic along with a cutting board and knife and slice them there, whichever is more convenient. In either case, transport spirals in a cooler.

EACH SLICE WITH SALMON FILLING
About 85 calories, 3g protein, 6g carbohydrate, 5g total fat (3g saturated), 0g fiber,
15mg cholesterol, 155mg sodium

EACH SLICE WITH TOMATO FILLING
About 85 calories, 3g protein, 7g carbohydrate, 5g total fat (3g saturated), 0g fiber,
13mg cholesterol, 155mg sodium

STUFFED EGGS

ACTIVE TIME 30 minutes · **TOTAL TIME** 10 minutes plus standing
MAKES 12 stuffed eggs

This is such a fun recipe—prepare all of one kind or get inspired and prepare a variety of fillings.

1 In 3-quart saucepan, place eggs and enough *cold water* to cover by at least 1 inch; heat to boiling over high heat. Immediately remove saucepan from heat and cover tightly; let stand 15 minutes. Pour off hot water and run cold water over eggs to cool. Peel eggs.

2 Slice eggs lengthwise in half. Gently remove yolks and place in medium bowl; with fork, finely mash yolks. Stir in mayonnaise, milk, and salt until evenly blended. Egg-yolk mixture and egg whites can be covered separately and refrigerated up to 24 hours.

3 Place egg whites in jelly-roll pan lined with paper towels (to prevent eggs from rolling). Spoon egg-yolk mixture into pastry bag fitted with star tip or zip-tight plastic bag with one corner cut off. Pipe about 1 tablespoon yolk mixture into each egg-white half, or simply spoon mixture. Cover eggs and refrigerate until thoroughly chilled, at least 1 hour and up to 4 hours.

6 large eggs
¼ cup mayonnaise
1 tablespoon milk
⅛ teaspoon salt

EACH STUFFED EGG
About 72 calories, 3g protein, 0g carbohydrate, 6g total fat (1g saturated), 0g fiber, 109mg cholesterol, 82mg sodium

Bacon-Horseradish Stuffed Eggs

Prepare as directed, left, but add **2 table-spoons crumbled crisp-cooked bacon** and **1 tablespoon bottled white horseradish** to yolk mixture. If not serving right away, sprinkle crumbled bacon on top of stuffed eggs instead of adding to yolk mixture.

EACH STUFFED EGG About 80 calories, 4g protein, 1g carbohydrate, 7g total fat (2g saturated), 0g fiber, 110mg cholesterol, 102mg sodium

Dried Tomato–Caper Stuffed Eggs

Prepare as directed, left, but add **1 table-spoon plus 2 teaspoons chopped dried tomatoes packed in herb-seasoned olive oil, 1 tablespoon plus 2 teaspoons chopped drained capers,** and **⅛ teaspoon coarsely ground black pepper** to yolk mixture.

EACH STUFFED EGG About 78 calories, 3g protein, 1g carbohydrate, 7g total fat (1g saturated), 0g fiber, 109mg cholesterol, 143mg sodium

Lemon-Basil Stuffed Eggs

Prepare as directed, left, but add **1 table-spoon chopped fresh basil, ¼ teaspoon grated lemon peel,** and **¼ teaspoon coarsely ground black pepper** to yolk mixture.

EACH STUFFED EGG About 73 calories, 3g protein, 0g carbohydrate, 6g total fat (1g saturated), 0g fiber, 109mg cholesterol, 82mg sodium

Pimiento-Studded Stuffed Eggs

Prepare as directed, left, but add **2 table-spoons chopped pimientos, 2 teaspoons Dijon mustard,** and **¼ teaspoon ground red pepper (cayenne)** to yolk mixture.

EACH STUFFED EGG About 74 calories, 3g protein, 1g carbohydrate, 6g total fat (1g saturated), 0g fiber, 109mg cholesterol, 102mg sodium

POTLUCK PREP If you're a stuffed-egg lover, we suggest you invest in a deviled egg carrier. They're widely available and come in a variety of styles. What they do is allow you to transport your stuffed eggs in a covered container designed to keep the eggs from rolling over. Set the carrier on freezer packs in a cooler to transport and bring plates (deviled egg trays, preferably) for serving.

BLACK BEAN DIP

ACTIVE TIME 5 minutes · **TOTAL TIME** 8 minutes plus chilling · **MAKES** 2 cups

Why purchase bean dip when it's so fast and easy to make? You can scale this recipe up as much as you need to for the number of guests you'll have coming.

1 In 1-quart saucepan, heat *2 cups water* to boiling over high heat. Add garlic and cook 3 minutes to blanch; drain.

2 In food processor with knife blade attached, combine garlic, beans, tomato paste, oil, lime juice, 1 tablespoon water, cumin, coriander, salt, and ground red pepper. Process until smooth.

3 Transfer to airtight container; cover and refrigerate up to 4 hours. Serve with tortilla chips.

4 garlic cloves, peeled

1 can (15 to 19 ounces) black beans, rinsed and drained

2 tablespoons tomato paste

2 tablespoons olive oil

4½ teaspoons fresh lime juice

1 tablespoon water

½ teaspoon ground cumin

½ teaspoon ground coriander

¼ teaspoon salt

⅛ teaspoon ground red pepper (cayenne)

tortilla chips

EACH TABLESPOON
About 18 calories, 1g protein, 2g carbohydrate, 1g total fat (0g saturated), 1g fiber, 0mg cholesterol, 50mg sodium

POTLUCK PREP Transport in a cooler in an airtight container, along with a serving bowl, chips, and a bowl or basket for the chips.

CAMPFIRE CORN WITH HERB BUTTER

ACTIVE TIME: 15 minutes plus soaking · TOTAL TIME 25 minutes
MAKES 12 side-dish servings

Leaving the husks on when roasting corn prevents the delicate kernels from drying out.

1 Prepare outdoor grill for direct grilling over medium heat.

2 Gently pull husks three-fourths of way down on each ear of corn; remove silk. In large kettle, place kitchen twine and corn with husks. Add enough *water* to cover; let soak for at least 15 minutes. (Soaking in water helps keep husks and twine from burning on grill.)

3 Meanwhile, in small bowl, stir shallot, butter, parsley, tarragon, lemon peel, salt, and pepper. Let stand at room temperature up to 20 minutes or refrigerate overnight, if you like.

4 Remove corn and twine from water; drain well. With pastry brush, brush each ear with some butter mixture. Pull husks back up and, with twine, tie them at top of ears.

5 Place corn on hot grill rack over medium heat. Grill, turning occasionally, until husks are brown and dry and kernels are tender, 20 to 30 minutes. Serve with lime wedges, if you like.

12 medium ears corn, with husks and silk

12 (8-inch) pieces kitchen twine

2 medium shallots, minced

6 tablespoons butter or margarine, softened

4 tablespoons minced fresh parsley

2 teaspoons minced fresh tarragon

2 teaspoons freshly grated lemon peel

1 teaspoon salt

2¼ teaspoons ground black pepper

lime wedges (optional)

EACH SERVING
About 140 calories, 3g protein, 20g carbohydrate, 7g total fat (4g saturated), 2g fiber, 16mg cholesterol, 252mg sodium

POTLUCK PREP Prepare herb butter the night before the party; transfer to a small airtight container and refrigerate. Soak and grill the corn at the party.

SWEET AND TANGY BARBECUE CHICKEN

ACTIVE TIME 15 minutes · **TOTAL TIME** 1 hour 30 minutes · **MAKES** 12 servings

This bold-flavored barbecue sauce can stand up to most anything you choose to slather it with—ribs, brisket, chops.

1 Prepare chicken: Preheat oven to 425°F. Arrange chicken quarters in large roasting pan (17" by 11½"), overlapping pieces if necessary. Sprinkle chicken with salt; top with lemon and onion wedges. Cover roasting pan tightly with heavy-duty foil. Oven-steam until juices run clear when thickest part of chicken is pierced with tip of knife, about 1 hour and 15 minutes, turning chicken over halfway through baking time to ensure even cooking. Discard lemons and onion. Refrigerate broth for use another day. Transfer chicken to large platter; cover and refrigerate until completely cold, at least 2 hours and up to overnight.

2 Meanwhile, prepare barbecue sauce: In 5- to 6-quart saucepot, heat oil over medium heat until hot. (Do not use a smaller pan; sauce bubbles up and splatters during cooking—the deeper the pot, the better.) Add chopped onion and cook until tender and golden, about 10 minutes, stirring occasionally. Add garlic and chili powder; cook

Oven-Steamed Chicken
3 chickens (4 pounds each), each cut into quarters, skin removed if you like

1½ teaspoons salt

2 lemons, cut into wedges

1 large onion (12 ounces), cut into wedges

1 minute. Remove saucepot from heat; carefully stir in tomato puree, apricot preserves, vinegar, mustard, Worcestershire sauce, and salt. Heat sauce to boiling over medium-low heat; cook, partially covered, 10 minutes to thicken slightly, stirring occasionally.

3 Transfer sauce to bowl; cover and refrigerate if not using right away. Sauce will keep up to 1 week in refrigerator or up to 2 months in freezer. Makes about 6 cups.

4 Prepare outdoor grill for covered direct grilling over medium heat.

5 Place chicken on hot grill rack; cover grill and cook 10 minutes, turning chicken over once. Reserve 3 cups barbecue sauce to serve with grilled chicken. Cook chicken, turning over occasionally and frequently brushing with remaining barbecue sauce, until chicken is heated through and sauce is browned, 5 to 10 minutes longer. If necessary, heat reserved barbecue sauce to serve with chicken.

Sweet and Tangy Barbecue Sauce

1 tablespoon olive oil

1 large onion (12 ounces), chopped

3 garlic cloves, crushed with garlic press

¼ cup chili powder

1 can (28 ounces) tomato puree

1 jar (12 ounces) apricot preserves

½ cup cider vinegar

3 tablespoons spicy brown mustard

2 tablespoons Worcestershire sauce

1 teaspoon salt

EACH SERVING BARBECUE CHICKEN
About 315 calories, 44g protein, 6g carbohydrate, 12g total fat (3g saturated), 0g fiber, 135mg cholesterol, 540mg sodium

POTLUCK PREP Prepare far enough in advance to allow time for proper chilling; to prevent any food safety issues, the chicken needs to be completely cold before you pack it for the picnic. Transport it in a cooler in large zip-tight plastic bags or a large covered rectangular glass dish. If you plan to serve barbecue sauce on the side with the chicken, heat it to boiling right before leaving and transport it in thermos bottles. Bring a bowl to pour some of it into for basting, along with a basting brush, and a serving bowl for the remainder. If you transport the chicken in bags, also bring a large serving platter for the finished chicken.

BRISKET WITH CHUNKY BARBECUE SAUCE

ACTIVE TIME 35 minutes · **TOTAL TIME** 4 hours · **MAKES** 12 servings

You can serve your brisket sliced, for people to pile onto their plates, as we suggest here, or you can chop the brisket up and pile it onto buns for brisket sandwiches.

1 Prepare brisket: In 8-quart Dutch oven, place brisket, onion quarters, carrot, bay leaf, peppercorns, and allspice. Add enough *water* to cover and heat to boiling over high heat. Reduce heat; cover and simmer until meat is tender, about 3 hours.

2 Meanwhile, prepare barbecue sauce: In 12-inch skillet, heat oil over medium heat until hot. Add chopped onion and cook until tender, about 10 minutes, stirring occasionally. Add garlic and ginger and cook 1 minute, stirring. Stir in cumin. Stir in tomatoes and their puree, chili sauce, vinegar, brown sugar, molasses, and dry mustard; heat to boiling over high heat. Reduce heat to medium-high; cook 5 minutes, stirring occasionally. In cup, mix cornstarch and water until blended. Stir mixture into sauce and cook until sauce boils and thickens, 1 to 2 minutes longer. Cover and refrigerate if not using right away. Makes about 4 cups.

Brisket

1 beef brisket (4½ pounds), well trimmed

1 medium onion, cut into quarters

1 large carrot, peeled and cut into 1½-inch pieces

1 bay leaf

1 teaspoon whole black peppercorns

¼ teaspoon whole allspice berries

EACH SERVING WITHOUT SAUCE
About 241 calories, 26g protein, 6g carbohydrate, 11g total fat (4g saturated), 1g fiber, 81mg cholesterol, 174mg sodium

3 When brisket is done, transfer to large platter. Cover and refrigerate until ready to serve.

4 Prepare outdoor grill for covered direct grilling over medium heat.

5 Place brisket on hot grill rack, cover, and cook 10 minutes. Turn brisket and cook 5 minutes longer. Spoon 1 cup barbecue sauce on top of brisket and cook until brisket is heated through, about 5 minutes longer. (Do not turn brisket after topping with sauce.) Transfer brisket to cutting board.

6 To serve, slice brisket thinly across the grain, transfer to serving platter, and serve with sauce.

Chunky Barbecue Sauce

1 tablespoon vegetable oil

1 large onion (12 ounces), chopped

3 garlic cloves, minced

2 tablespoons minced, peeled fresh ginger

1 teaspoon ground cumin

1 can (14½ ounces) tomatoes in puree, chopped, puree reserved

1 bottle (12 ounces) chili sauce

⅓ cup cider vinegar

2 tablespoons brown sugar

2 tablespoons light (mild) molasses

2 teaspoons dry mustard

1 tablespoon cornstarch

2 tablespoons water

EACH ¼ CUP SAUCE
About 61 calories, 1g protein, 13g carbohydrate, 1g total fat (0g saturated), 1g fiber, 0mg cholesterol, 328mg sodium

POTLUCK PREP Transport precooked brisket in a cooler, wrapped in foil or in a zip-tight plastic bag. Heat barbecue sauce to boiling right before leaving and transport in thermos bottles. Bring a bowl to pour some sauce in for basting, as well as a basting brush, and a serving bowl for the remainder. If you're not at someone's home, bring a cutting board and chef's knife, as well as a serving platter.

RIBS SUPREME

The secret ingredient in the secret-recipe barbecue sauce is pineapple.

1 Preheat oven to 350°F.

2 In cup, mix grated ginger, lemon peel, salt, and garlic cloves until combined. Rub ginger mixture all over ribs.

3 Place ribs in large roasting pan (15½" by 11½"), overlapping slightly. Pour *2 cups boiling water* into roasting pan. Cover pan tightly with foil. Steam ribs 1 hour.

4 Meanwhile, prepare barbecue sauce: In 5- to 6-quart saucepot, heat oil over medium heat until hot. (Do not use a smaller pot; sauce bubbles up and splatters during cooking—the deeper the pot, the better.) Add onion and chopped ginger; cook until onion is tender and golden, about 10 minutes, stirring occasionally. Add chili powder; cook 1 minute, stirring. Add garlic and pineapple with its juice and cook 1 minute longer. Remove pot from heat. Stir in tomatoes, ketchup, vinegar, brown sugar, molasses, dry mustard, and salt. Spoon one-fourth of sauce into blender. At low speed, puree until smooth.

Oven-Steamed Ribs

4 teaspoons grated, peeled fresh ginger

2 teaspoons freshly grated lemon peel

¾ teaspoon salt

2 garlic cloves, crushed with garlic press

4 racks (1 pound each) pork baby back ribs

Pour sauce into bowl; repeat with remaining sauce.

5 Return sauce to saucepot; heat to boiling over high heat. Reduce heat to medium-low and cook, partially covered, until reduced to about 5 cups, about 25 minutes, stirring occasionally. Cover and refrigerate if not using right away. Sauce will keep up to 1 week in refrigerator or up to 2 months in freezer. You will need about 2 cups sauce for this recipe.

6 Carefully remove foil from roasting pan (escaping steam is very hot). Remove ribs from roasting pan; discard water. Ribs can be refrigerated up to 2 days before grilling.

7 Prepare outdoor grill for direct grilling over medium heat.

8 Place ribs, meat side up, on hot grill rack and cook 5 minutes, turning once. Turn ribs over, brush with some barbecue sauce and grill 5 minutes. Turn ribs over again, brush with more sauce, and grill 5 minutes longer.

9 Cut racks into 2-rib portions and serve with additional sauce alongside.

Secret-Recipe Barbecue Sauce

1 tablespoon olive oil

1 large (12 ounces) onion, chopped

2 tablespoons chopped, peeled fresh ginger

3 tablespoons chili powder

3 garlic cloves, crushed with garlic press

1 can (8 ounces) crushed pineapple in juice

1 can (28 ounces) crushed tomatoes

1/3 cup ketchup

1/4 cup cider vinegar

3 tablespoons dark brown sugar

3 tablespoons light (mild) molasses

2 teaspoons dry mustard

1 teaspoon salt

EACH SERVING RIBS SUPREME
About 615 calories, 36g protein, 16g carbohydrate, 44g total fat (16g saturated), 0g fiber, 172mg cholesterol, 760mg sodium

POTLUCK PREP Transport precooked ribs in a cooler wrapped in foil or in zip-tight plastic bags. Heat barbecue sauce to boiling right before leaving and transport in thermos bottles. Bring a bowl to pour some sauce in for basting, as well as a basting brush, and a serving bowl for the remainder. Also bring a cutting board, chef's knife, and serving platter.

CLOCKWISE FROM LEFT Creamy Cucumber-Dill Salad; Antipasto Salad; Chunky Greek Salad (recipes pages 65–67)

CREAMY CUCUMBER-DILL SALAD

TOTAL TIME 35 minutes plus standing and chilling
MAKES 5 cups or 10 side-dish servings

This creamy, cool, and crunchy salad is a summertime classic. Don't skip the salting step or the cukes will be limp, not crisp.

1 With vegetable peeler, remove several strips of peel from each cucumber. Cut each cucumber lengthwise in half; with teaspoon, scoop out seeds. With knife or in food processor fitted with slicing blade, thinly slice cucumber halves crosswise. In large bowl, toss cucumbers with salt; let stand 30 minutes.

2 Meanwhile, thinly slice radishes; transfer to serving bowl. Add yogurt, sour cream, dill, lime juice, pepper, and garlic. Stir until well combined.

3 Transfer sliced cucumbers to a colander. With hands, press cucumbers over sink to remove as much liquid as possible. Pat cucumbers dry with paper towels.

4 Add cucumbers to bowl with yogurt mixture. Toss until evenly coated. Cover and refrigerate at least 1 hour or overnight to blend flavors.

8 large (about 5 pounds) cucumbers

1 teaspoon salt

6 large radishes

1 container (8 ounces) plain low-fat yogurt

½ cup reduced-fat sour cream

½ cup loosely packed fresh dill, chopped

2 tablespoons fresh lime juice

¼ teaspoon ground black pepper

1 small garlic clove, crushed with garlic press

EACH SERVING
About 60 calories, 3g protein, 9g carbohydrate, 2g total fat (1g saturated), 2g fiber, 6mg cholesterol, 180mg sodium

POTLUCK PREP Prepare far enough in advance to allow time for proper chilling. Transport in a cooler in covered serving bowl with serving spoon.

ANTIPASTO SALAD

ACTIVE TIME 15 minutes · **TOTAL TIME** 20 minutes
YIELD 15 cups or 20 side-dish servings

Antipasto means "before the pasta" in Italian. Here you get to serve the pasta plus salami, fresh mozzarella, and an assortment of marinated vegetables, all in one big salad bowl. If you can't locate boccocino (sold in Italian delis and many supermarkets), use one 16-ounce package mozzarella cheese cut into ¾-inch cubes.

1 Heat large covered saucepot of salted *water* to boiling over high heat. Add pasta and cook as label directs.

2 Meanwhile, in small bowl, combine onion and ½ cup *very hot water*; let soak 5 minutes.

3 Drain pasta. Rinse with cold running water to stop cooking; drain again. Drain onion.

4 In large serving bowl, combine pasta, onion, mozzarella, salami, tomatoes, artichokes, olives, pimientos, oil, vinegar, salt, and pepper. Toss until evenly mixed. Chill before serving.

1 package (16 ounces) corkscrew pasta (rotini)

1 red onion, cut in half and very thinly sliced

1 pound small fresh mozzarella cheese balls (bocconcino)

10 ounces hard salami in 1 piece, cut into ¾-inch cubes (2 cups)

1 pint cherry or grape tomatoes, each cut in half

1 can (13¾ to 14 ounces) quartered artichoke hearts in brine, drained

1 can (2¼ ounces) sliced black olives, drained

1 jar (4 ounces) sliced pimientos, drained

⅓ cup olive oil

⅓ cup red wine vinegar

1½ teaspoons salt

coarsely ground black pepper to taste

EACH SERVING
About 255 calories, 11g protein, 21g carbohydrate, 14g total fat (5g saturated), 1g fiber, 29mg cholesterol, 550mg sodium

POTLUCK PREP Feel free to make this the night before: The veggies and mozzarella will marinate in the vinaigrette.

CHUNKY GREEK SALAD

TOTAL TIME 30 minutes · **MAKES** 8 cups or 12 side-dish servings

This salad is a pretty combination of ripe summer tomatoes, chunks of tangy feta cheese, and garden mint.

1 In large serving bowl, with wire whisk, mix oil, lemon juice, salt, and black pepper.

2 Add tomatoes, cucumbers, red pepper, green onion, olives, and mint. Toss until evenly mixed. Cover and refrigerate up to 6 hours.

3 Right before serving, sprinkle with feta if using. Toss again before serving.

2 tablespoons olive oil

2 tablespoons fresh lemon juice

¾ teaspoon salt

½ teaspoon coarsely ground black pepper

1 pint cherry or grape tomatoes, each cut in half

6 Kirby cucumbers (about 1½ pounds), unpeeled, cut into 1" by ½" chunks

1 large red pepper, cut into 1-inch pieces

1 green onion, thinly sliced

½ cup Kalamata olives, pitted and coarsely chopped

¼ cup loosely packed fresh mint leaves, chopped

¾ cup crumbled feta cheese (3 ounces; optional)

EACH SERVING
About 45 calories, 1g protein, 5g carbohydrate, 3g total fat (0g saturated), 2g fiber, 0mg cholesterol, 195mg sodium

POTLUCK PREP Cover the salad and put the crumbled feta cheese in a small zip-tight plastic bag; bring salad tongs. Right before serving, toss feta with salad.

S'MORE BARS

ACTIVE TIME 15 minutes · **TOTAL TIME** 1 hour 5 minutes · **MAKES** 24 bars

Just as yummy as the campfire original—but easier to transport!

1 Preheat oven to 350°F. Grease and flour 13" by 9" metal baking pan. Coarsely crumble enough graham crackers to equal 1 cup pieces; set aside. With rolling pin, crush remaining graham crackers to equal ½ cup fine crumbs. In medium bowl, with wire whisk, mix flour, baking powder, salt, and finely crushed graham-cracker crumbs.

2 In heavy 3-quart saucepan, melt butter over low heat. Remove saucepan from heat. With wooden spoon, stir in brown and granulated sugars and vanilla, then stir in eggs until well blended. Add flour mixture and stir just until blended. Stir in nuts.

3 Spread batter evenly in prepared pan. Bake until top is lightly golden, 30 minutes. Remove pan from oven and sprinkle with graham-cracker pieces, chocolate pieces, and marshmallows. Bake 10 minutes longer, or until marshmallows are puffed and golden. Cool completely in pan on wire rack. When cool, cut lengthwise into 4 strips, then cut each strip crosswise into 6 pieces.

8 graham crackers
(5" by 2½" each)

1½ cup all-purpose flour

2¼ teaspoons baking powder

1 teaspoon salt

¾ cup (1½ sticks) butter or margarine, softened

1 cup (packed) light brown sugar

¾ cup granulated sugar

1 tablespoon vanilla extract

4 large eggs

1 cup walnuts or pecans, coarsely chopped

1 bar (7- to 8-ounce) semisweet or milk chocolate, cut into small pieces

2 cups mini marshmallows

EACH BAR
About 260 calories, 3g protein, 36g carbohydrate, 12g total fat (2g saturated), 0g fiber, 36mg cholesterol, 250mg sodium

POTLUCK PREP Transport in cookie tins, separating each layer with waxed paper.

PEANUT BUTTER AND JELLY BARS

ACTIVE TIME 20 minutes · **TOTAL TIME** 50 minutes · **MAKES** 42 bars

Here peanut butter and jelly are transformed into a yummy dessert bar.

1 Preheat oven to 350°F.

2 In large bowl, with mixer on medium speed, beat sugar, peanut butter, butter, vanilla, and egg until blended. Increase speed to high; beat until light and fluffy, about 1 minute, scraping down bowl occasionally with rubber spatula.

3 Reduce speed to low; add flour, oats, and baking soda and beat just until blended. Transfer 4 cups of peanut butter mixture to 15½" by 10½" jelly-roll pan. With fingertips, firmly press mixture into bottom of pan to form crust. Spread with jelly up to ¼ inch from edges. Sprinkle remaining peanut butter mixture over jelly.

4 Bake until top browns slightly, 30 to 35 minutes. Cool completely in pan on wire rack. When cool, cut lengthwise into 6 strips, then cut each strip crosswise into 7 bars.

1 cup sugar

1 cup creamy peanut butter

½ cup butter or margarine (1 stick), softened

2 teaspoons vanilla extract

1 large egg

2 cups all-purpose flour

1½ cups old-fashioned or quick-cooking oats, uncooked

½ teaspoon baking soda

1 jar (12 to 13 ounces) favorite jelly, jam, or preserves (about 1 cup)

EACH BAR
About 145 calories, 3g protein, 20g carbohydrate, 6g total fat (2g saturated), 1g fiber, 11mg cholesterol, 70mg sodium

POTLUCK PREP Transport in cookie tins, separating each layer with waxed paper.

NEIGHBORHOOD
Fourth of July Fun

Lemon-Limeade

Lemon-Cilantro
Eggplant Dip

Garden-Fresh Chopped Salad
with Herb-Ranch Dressing

Creamy Potato Salad

Grilled Buffalo Drumsticks

Mini Burgers with
Choice of Flavored Mayos

Rich Stovetop Baked Beans

Almond-Berry Cheesecake
Tart

Whoopie Pies

A July Fourth celebration is the perfect excuse to invite the neighbors over. We recommend classic fare with a twist. Instead of Buffalo wings, enjoy grilled drumsticks glazed with hot sauce and creamy blue cheese dip. For burgers, we've given you three flavor options plus a trio of mayonnaise toppings. Potato salad and baked beans are straight-up traditional, and we've also included a refreshing chopped salad. Round out the meal with red, white, and blue—blueberries and strawberries set on the creamy backdrop of a cheesecake tart. And for the kids, what could be more fun than whoopie pies?

LEMON-LIMEADE

ACTIVE TIME 20 minutes · **TOTAL TIME** 25 minutes plus chilling time
MAKES 12 servings

What is the Fourth of July without lemonade? This summer cooler throws limes and seltzer into the mix. If the kids want to assist with party prep, this is the perfect recipe. Depending on their age, you may want to peel the citrus strips before they get started on juicing.

2 cups sugar

4 cups cold water

8 lemons

8 limes

2 cups seltzer

EACH SERVING
About 140 calories, 0g protein, 36g carbohydrate, 0g fat, 0g fiber, 0mg cholesterol, 1g sodium

1 Combine sugar and 2 cups water in small saucepan. Bring to simmer, stirring, until sugar is dissolved. Remove from heat.

2 With vegetable peeler, remove 12 (2-inch) strips peel from 8 lemons; remove 12 strips peel from 8 limes. Squeeze lemons to get ½ cup juice; squeeze limes to get 1 cup juice; set aside.

3 Add lemon and lime peels and remaining 2 cups cold water to pan. Transfer to a pitcher; cover and chill at least 2 hours.

4 Slice 2 lemons and 2 limes. Stir into pitcher along with sugar mixture, lemon juice, lime juice, and seltzer. Serve in ice-filled glasses.

POTLUCK PREP Prepare through step 3 far enough in advance to allow proper chilling. Bring the combined lemon and lime juices in an airtight container, the lemon and lime slices in a zip-tight plastic bag, and the seltzer, as well as a pitcher. Combine everything in the pitcher at the potluck.

LEMON-CILANTRO EGGPLANT DIP

ACTIVE TIME 10 minutes · **TOTAL TIME** 55 minutes plus chilling · **MAKES** 2 cups

The rich, smoky taste of the roasted eggplant coupled with the citrus punch of the lemon juice and cilantro makes this an unexpected but perfect pairing with the grilled chicken drumsticks and burgers.

1 Preheat oven to 450°F. Line 15½" by 10½" jelly-roll pan with nonstick foil (or use regular foil and spray with nonstick cooking spray). Place eggplant halves, skin side up, in foil-lined pan. Wrap garlic in foil and place in pan with eggplants. Roast until eggplants are very tender and skin is shriveled and browned, 45 to 50 minutes. Unwrap garlic. Cool eggplants and garlic until easy to handle.

2 When cool, scoop eggplants' flesh into food processor with knife blade attached. Squeeze out garlic pulp from each clove and add to food processor with tahini, lemon juice, and salt; pulse to coarsely chop. Spoon dip into serving bowl; stir in cilantro. Cover and refrigerate at least 2 hours.

3 Serve dip with pita and vegetables.

2 eggplants (1 pound each), each halved lengthwise

4 garlic cloves, unpeeled

3 tablespoons tahini (sesame puree)

3 tablespoons fresh lemon juice

¾ teaspoon salt

¼ cup loosely packed fresh cilantro or mint leaves, chopped

toasted or grilled pita strips

carrot and cucumber sticks and red or yellow pepper slices

EACH SERVING
About 10 calories, 0g protein, 2g carbohydrate, 0g fat, 1g fiber, 0mg cholesterol, 55mg sodium

POTLUCK PREP Make dip earlier in the day to allow time for proper chilling. Transport in a covered container and the cut-up veggies in a zip-tight plastic bag. Bring a platter and serving bowl. Toast the pitas on the grill or under the broiler at the potluck and cut into strips.

GARDEN-FRESH CHOPPED SALAD WITH HERB-RANCH DRESSING

TOTAL TIME 30 minutes · **MAKES** 14 cups or 8 side-dish servings

This is a stunner of a layered salad, best shown off in a deep glass bowl.

1   Heat 3-quart saucepan of *water* to boiling over high heat. Add green beans and cook until tender-crisp, about 5 minutes. Drain in colander and rinse under cold running water to stop cooking.

2   Meanwhile, in medium bowl, whisk buttermilk, mayonnaise, vinegar, chives, parsley, green onion, salt, and pepper until blended; set dressing aside.

3   In 4-quart or larger cylindrical glass bowl or trifle dish (large enough to toss salad), place half of chopped lettuce, then half of tomatoes; top with all of green beans, all of peppers, remaining lettuce, then remaining tomatoes. Arrange avocados on top. Spoon dressing over avocados to cover completely. Cover bowl tightly with plastic wrap and refrigerate salad until ready to serve or up to 4 hours.

4   Right before serving, toss salad until well coated with dressing.

1 pound green beans, trimmed and cut into 1-inch pieces

1/2 cup buttermilk

1/3 cup light mayonnaise

2 tablespoons cider vinegar

2 tablespoons snipped fresh chives

2 tablespoons chopped fresh parsley

1 green onion, minced

1/2 teaspoon salt

1/4 teaspoon coarsely ground black pepper

8 ounces hearts of romaine lettuce, coarsely chopped

4 pints red and/or yellow cherry tomatoes, each cut in half

2 red, orange, and/or yellow peppers, cut into 1-inch pieces

2 avocados, pitted, peeled, and cut into 1/2-inch chunks

EACH SERVING
About 185 calories, 5g protein, 20g carbohydrate, 12g total fat (2g saturated), 0g fiber, 0mg cholesterol, 50mg sodium

POTLUCK PREP If traveling any distance, transport in a cooler. Toss salad at potluck. Bring two large spoons or salad forks for tossing and salad tongs for serving.

CREAMY POTATO SALAD

ACTIVE TIME 10 minutes · **TOTAL TIME** 45 minutes plus standing and chilling
MAKES 10 side-dish servings

You can't go wrong with a classic like this one. The cider vinegar and brown mustard offer a nice sharp counterpoint to the creaminess of the potatoes and mayonnaise.

1 In 4-quart saucepan, place potatoes, 2 teaspoons salt, and enough *water* to cover; heat to boiling over high heat. Reduce heat to low; cover and simmer until potatoes are fork-tender, 10 to 15 minutes. Drain; cool slightly.

2 Meanwhile, in large serving bowl, combine vinegar, sugar, mustard, pepper, mayonnaise, and remaining ½ teaspoon salt.

3 When potatoes are cool enough to handle, cut each into quarters or eighths if large. Add celery and warm potatoes to dressing in bowl; gently stir with rubber spatula until well coated. Let potato mixture stand 30 minutes to absorb dressing, stirring occasionally.

4 Cover and refrigerate until completely cold, at least 2 hours and up to 1 day.

4 pounds medium red potatoes, unpeeled

2½ teaspoons salt

⅓ cup cider vinegar

1 tablespoon sugar

1 tablespoon spicy brown mustard

¼ teaspoon ground black pepper

½ cup mayonnaise

2 stalks celery, thinly sliced crosswise

EACH SERVING
About 200 calories, 3g protein, 32g carbohydrate, 8g total fat (1g saturated), 3g fiber, 5mg cholesterol, 275mg sodium

POTLUCK PREP Prepare in advance to allow time for proper chilling. Transport in covered serving bowl in a cooler if traveling a distance.

GRILLED BUFFALO DRUMSTICKS

ACTIVE TIME 20 minutes · **TOTAL TIME** 50 minutes · **MAKES** 8 drumsticks

This is an easy recipe to adapt to the number of guests coming. Figure on two drumsticks for those who won't be having a burger, and one for everyone else.

1 Prepare dipping sauce: In bowl, with wire whisk, mix sauce ingredients until well combined. Cover and refrigerate until ready to use or up to 3 days. Makes about 1 cup.

2 Prepare outdoor grill for covered direct grilling over medium heat.

3 Place drumsticks on hot grill rack. Cover grill and cook until browned, about 25 minutes, turning over occasionally. Brush drumsticks generously with some cayenne pepper sauce. Cook until drumsticks are glazed and juices run clear when thickest part of each drumstick is pierced with tip of knife, 5 to 7 minutes longer, brushing with remaining sauce and turning frequently.

4 Arrange drumsticks on platter. Serve with dipping sauce and celery and carrot sticks.

Blue Cheese Dipping Sauce

1/2 cup sour cream

1/3 cup light mayonnaise

1/2 cup crumbled blue cheese

1 tablespoon cider vinegar

1/2 teaspoon Worcestershire sauce

1/4 teaspoon salt

1 green onion, finely chopped

EACH TABLESPOON SAUCE
About 45 calories, 1g protein, 1g carbohydrate, 4g total fat (2g saturated), 0g fiber, 7mg cholesterol, 120mg sodium

Buffalo Drumsticks

8 large chicken drumsticks (about 2 1/2 pounds)

1/2 cup cayenne pepper sauce

celery and carrot sticks

TWO DRUMSTICKS WITHOUT SAUCE
About 275 calories, 34g protein, 1g carbohydrate, 14g total fat (4g saturated), 0g fiber, 114mg cholesterol, 340mg sodium

POTLUCK PREP Transport dipping sauce in an airtight container along with a serving bowl, celery and carrot sticks in a zip-tight plastic bag, and uncooked drumsticks in a separate bag. Also bring a large platter and a bottle of cayenne sauce for basting.

MINI BURGERS WITH A TRIO OF FLAVORED MAYOS

ACTIVE TIME 10 minutes · **TOTAL TIME** 20 minutes
MAKES 12 mini burgers or 4 large burgers

These burgers are a great choice for a backyard get-together. Serve as homemade sliders or as regular-size burgers. For even more fun, prepare all three versions, along with the flavored mayos on pages 82–83, setting out labels so your guests can mix and match.

If preparing any of the burgers with ground chicken or turkey, make sure to spray both sides of the patties with nonstick spray and cook until the internal temperature reaches 170°F, 6 to 7 minutes for minis (12 to 14 minutes for large burgers).

1 Prepare outdoor grill for direct grilling over medium heat.

2 Shape beef into twelve ½-inch-thick mini burgers or four ¾-inch-thick large burgers. Sprinkle burgers with salt and pepper to season both sides.

3 Place burgers on hot grill rack; cook mini burgers 5 to 6 minutes, large burgers 10 to 12 minutes for medium or until desired doneness, turning over once. Burgers should reach an internal temperature of 160°F.

1¼ pounds ground beef chuck

¾ teaspoon salt

½ teaspoon ground black pepper

12 mini potato rolls, mini pitas, or other small buns, split

plum tomato slices, small lettuce leaves, dill pickle slices, and/or onion slices (optional)

choice of flavored mayos (pages 82–83; optional)

EACH MINI BURGER
About 145 calories, 10g protein, 9g carbohydrate, 8g total fat (3g saturated), 1g fiber, 32mg cholesterol, 240mg sodium

4 Serve burgers with rolls, tomato, lettuce, pickles, onion, and choice of flavored mayonnaise, if you like.

Corn and Salsa Burgers

Prepare Mini Burgers as directed, left, with ground chicken or turkey, but in step 2, before shaping burgers, mix in **½ cup fresh or frozen (thawed) corn kernels** and **¼ cup medium salsa** until blended, but do not overmix. Do not sprinkle burgers with salt and pepper. At the end of step 3, place **slices of jalapeño Jack cheese (about 4 ounces total)** on top of burgers; cover grill and cook until cheese melts, about 1 minute longer. Serve burgers as in step 4, but instead of mayo, spoon **additional salsa** over burgers.

Teriyaki Burgers

Prepare Mini Burgers as directed, left, with ground beef, pork, chicken, or turkey, but in step 2, before shaping burgers, mix in **½ cup diced water chestnuts**, **¼ cup teriyaki sauce**, and **¼ teaspoon crushed red pepper** until blended, but do not overmix. Do not sprinkle burgers with salt and black pepper. Serve burgers as in step 4, but instead of a mayonnaise topping, divide **¼ cup hoisin sauce** to spoon evenly over burgers.

EACH MINI CORN AND SALSA BURGER
About 160 calories, 12g protein, 11g carbohydrate, 8g total fat (2g saturated), 1g fiber, 10mg cholesterol, 170mg sodium

EACH MINI TERIYAKI BURGER
About 165 calories, 11g protein, 13g carbohydrate, 8g total fat (3g saturated), 1g fiber, 32mg cholesterol, 410mg sodium

POTLUCK PREP We recommend that the host take responsibility for the burgers to avoid guests having to transport ground raw meat in warm weather.

ONION-THYME MAYO

TOTAL TIME 15 minutes · **MAKES** ½ cup

1 Prepare outdoor grill for direct grilling over medium heat. Place onion slices on hot grill rack and cook until tender and browned on both sides, 8 to 10 minutes, turning over once.

2 Transfer onion to cutting board; coarsely chop. Place onion in small serving bowl; stir in mayonnaise and thyme until blended. Refrigerate until needed.

1 medium onion, cut crosswise into ½-inch-thick rounds

¼ cup light mayonnaise

1 teaspoon fresh thyme leaves, chopped

EACH TABLESPOON
About 30 calories, 0g protein, 2g carbohydrate, 3g total fat (1g saturated), 0g fiber, 3mg cholesterol, 60mg sodium

HORSERADISH-MUSTARD MAYO

TOTAL TIME 5 minutes · **MAKES** ⅓ cup

In small serving bowl, combine mayonnaise, horseradish, and mustard; stir until blended. Refrigerate until needed.

¼ cup light mayonnaise

1 tablespoon bottled white horseradish

2 teaspoons Dijon mustard with seeds

EACH TABLESPOON
About 45 calories, 0g protein, 1g carbohydrate, 4g total fat (1g saturated), 0g fiber, 4mg cholesterol, 105mg sodium

BACON-CHIPOTLE MAYO

TOTAL TIME 10 minutes · **MAKES** ⅓ cup

1 Place bacon on paper-towel-lined microwave-safe plate. Cover with paper towel. Cook in microwave on High 1½ to 3 minutes, until well browned. Cool bacon until crisp.

2 Crumble bacon; place in small serving bowl. Stir in mayonnaise and chile puree until blended. Refrigerate until needed.

2 slices bacon

¼ cup light mayonnaise

1 teaspoon canned chipotle chile puree (adobo)

EACH TABLESPOON
About 55 calories, 1g protein, 1g carbohydrate, 5g total fat (1g saturated), 0g fiber, 6mg cholesterol, 135 mg sodium

RICH STOVETOP BAKED BEANS

ACTIVE TIME 10 minutes · **TOTAL TIME** about 30 minutes
MAKES 4½ cups or 8 side-dish servings

Baked beans are a potluck classic.

1 In 3-quart saucepan, cook bacon, onion, and pepper over medium heat until vegetables are lightly browned and almost tender, 8 to 10 minutes, stirring occasionally. Stir in ketchup, molasses, brown sugar, mustard, and ¼ teaspoon salt; cook 2 to 3 minutes to blend flavors.

2 Stir beans into mixture in saucepan. Reduce heat to medium-low and cook, uncovered, until sauce is thick and syrupy, about 20 minutes, stirring occasionally.

2 slices bacon, chopped

1 medium onion, chopped

1 green pepper, chopped

¼ cup ketchup

¼ cup dark molasses

¼ cup packed dark brown sugar

1 tablespoon dry mustard

3 cans (15 to 16 ounces each) pinto beans, drained

EACH SERVING
About 265 calories, 9g protein, 43g carbohydrate, 7g total fat (2g saturated), 8g fiber, 6mg cholesterol, 525mg sodium

ALMOND-BERRY CHEESECAKE TART

ACTIVE TIME 30 minutes · **TOTAL TIME** 30 minutes plus chilling · **MAKES** 10 servings

This tart is an elegant and scrumptious way to celebrate the red, white, and blue.

1 Preheat oven to 375°F.

2 Prepare crust: In food processor with knife blade attached, pulse almonds with sugar until finely ground; add graham crackers and pulse until fine crumbs form. Pour in melted butter; pulse until moistened. With hand, press mixture firmly onto bottom and up side of 11-inch tart pan with removable bottom. Bake crust 10 minutes. Cool on wire rack.

3 Reset oven control to 350°F. Prepare filling: In medium bowl, with mixer on low speed, beat cream cheese and sugar until smooth, occasionally scraping bowl with rubber spatula. Add eggs and vanilla, and almond extracts; beat just until combined.

4 Pour cheese mixture into cooled crust. Bake until set, about 20 minutes.

5 Cool tart on wire rack. Cover and refrigerate tart at least 2 hours.

6 To serve, arrange berries on top of tart.

Graham-Cracker Crust
1/2 cup slivered almonds

1 tablespoon sugar

11 graham crackers, broken in half

6 tablespoons butter or margarine, melted

Cheese Filling
1 1/2 packages (12 ounces total) cream cheese, softened

1/2 cup sugar

2 large eggs

1/4 teaspoon vanilla extract

1/4 teaspoon almond extract

1 pint fresh blueberries

1 pint fresh raspberries

EACH SLICE
About 285 calories, 5g protein, 21g carbohydrate, 21g total fat (11g saturated), 1g fiber, 83mg cholesterol, 235mg sodium

POTLUCK PREP Prepare far enough in advance to allow proper chilling time. Transport in tart pan in a cooler if traveling any distance. Keep refrigerated until ready to serve; remove tart ring before slicing.

WHOOPIE PIES

ACTIVE TIME 10 minutes · **TOTAL TIME** about 30 minutes
MAKES 4½ cups or 8 side-dish servings

These are especially for the kids, but you'll find a lot of grown-ups sneaking them off the plate!

1 Preheat oven to 350°F. Grease 2 large cookie sheets.

2 Prepare cookie dough: In large bowl, with wooden spoon, mix dough ingredients until smooth. Drop dough by heaping tablespoons, 2 inches apart, on each prepared cookie sheet. (There will be 12 rounds per sheet.)

3 Bake, rotating sheets between upper and lower racks halfway through baking, until cookies are puffy and toothpick inserted in center comes out clean, 12 to 14 minutes. With wide spatula, transfer cookies to wire racks to cool completely.

4 Prepare marshmallow filling: In large bowl, with mixer on medium speed, beat butter until smooth. Reduce speed to low; gradually beat in confectioners' sugar. Beat in marshmallow creme and vanilla until smooth.

5 Spread 1 rounded tablespoon filling on flat side of 12 cookies. Top with remaining cookies.

Cookie Dough

2 cups all-purpose flour

1 cup granulated sugar

¾ cup milk

½ cup unsweetened cocoa

6 tablespoons butter or margarine, melted

1 teaspoon baking soda

1 teaspoon vanilla extract

¼ teaspoon salt

1 large egg

Marshmallow Creme Filling

6 tablespoons butter or margarine, slightly softened

1 cup confectioners' sugar

1 jar (7 to 7½ ounces) marshmallow creme

1 teaspoon vanilla extract

EACH WHOOPIE PIE
365 calories, 4g protein, 59g carbohydrate, 14g total fat (8g saturated), 1.5g fiber, 51mg cholesterol, 290 mg sodium

POTLUCK PREP Transport in a cookie tin, separating the pies into layers with sheets of wax paper.

Dinner on the Lawn
PICNIC

—— MENU ——

Bruschetta with Tomatoes and Basil

Picnic Chicken Salad with Maple Vinaigrette

Honeydew and Lime Soup

Seafood Salad

Fresh Fruit with Raspberry-Lime Dipping Sauce

Summer provides so many lovely opportunities for a picnic. One of the best is attending an outdoor performance, whether it be a concert or a play or a movie. In most cases, the grounds are opened several hours beforehand to give event-goers the chance to enjoy a picnic dinner. This menu is tailor-made for just such an outdoor potluck. Every dish is prepared in advance and enjoyed cold or at room temperature. If you like, you can supplement the menu with a cheese selection, olives, or a store-bought pâté or smoked sausage.

BRUSCHETTA WITH TOMATOES AND BASIL

ACTIVE TIME 15 minutes · **TOTAL TIME** 30 minutes · **MAKES** 8 servings

Nothing can beat the simplicity and incredible flavor of homemade bruschetta topped with vine-ripened tomatoes. Look for locally grown tomatoes for the best flavor.

1 Preheat oven to 350°F. Meanwhile, slice bread diagonally into ½-inch-thick slices; reserve ends for making bread crumbs. Place bread slices on 2 cookie sheets.

2 Toast bread on 2 oven racks until crusty and dry, about 15 minutes, turning slices over once and rotating cookie sheets between upper and lower racks halfway through baking. Transfer bread to wire racks to cool slightly. When bread is cool enough to handle, rub 1 side of each toast slice with cut side of garlic. Discard garlic.

3 Meanwhile, in small bowl, gently toss tomatoes, basil, oil, salt, and pepper until combined.

4 To serve, spoon 1 heaping tablespoon tomato mixture on garlic-rubbed side of each toast slice.

1 loaf (8 ounces) Italian bread

1 large garlic clove, cut in half

1¼ pounds (8 medium) ripe plum tomatoes, seeded and cut into ¼-inch pieces

2 tablespoons thinly sliced fresh basil

2 tablespoons extra-virgin olive oil

¼ teaspoon salt

⅛ teaspoon ground black pepper

EACH SERVING
About 115 calories, 3g protein, 17g carbohydrate, 5g total fat (1g saturated), 2g fiber, 0mg cholesterol, 235mg sodium

POTLUCK PREP Prepare tomato topping right before leaving (refrigeration would dull its flavor). Bring a serving platter and transport topping and toasts separately in an airtight container and zip-tight plastic bag. Spoon topping onto the toasts when you're ready to serve to keep the toasts crisp.

PICNIC CHICKEN SALAD WITH MAPLE VINAIGRETTE

ACTIVE TIME 35 minutes · **TOTAL TIME** 1 hour · **MAKES** 12 main-dish servings

This is a salad showstopper, a generous bounty of crisp-cooked vegetables, tender baby spinach, crunchy cukes and radishes, and juicy tomatoes, coupled with pan-seared chicken breasts and bits of bacon.

1 In nonstick 12-inch skillet over medium heat, cook bacon until browned, stirring occasionally. With slotted spoon, transfer bacon to paper towels to drain. Discard bacon fat, but do not wipe skillet clean.

2 Meanwhile, heat 4-quart covered saucepan of *salted water* to boiling over high heat. Add asparagus; heat to boiling. After water returns to boiling, with slotted spoon, transfer asparagus to large bowl of ice water to stop cooking. Drain asparagus well; set aside.

3 Heat water remaining in saucepan to boiling over high heat. Add green beans; heat to boiling. After water returns to boiling, with slotted spoon, transfer beans to same bowl of ice water (adding more ice if necessary) to stop cooking. Drain beans well; set aside.

4 Heat same 12-inch skillet over medium-high heat until hot but not smoking. Add

(cont.)

Picnic Chicken Salad

1 pound sliced bacon, cut crosswise into 1-inch-wide pieces

1 bunch asparagus (about 1 pound), trimmed and cut into 2-inch pieces

12 ounces green beans, trimmed

2 pounds skinless, boneless chicken-breast halves (about 6 medium)

1 bag (5 to 6 ounces) baby spinach, baby romaine, arugula, or watercress (about 8 cups)

1 small seedless cucumber or 3 Kirby (pickling) cucumbers, unpeeled, thinly sliced

1 pint grape or cherry tomatoes, each cut in half

1 cup frozen peas, thawed

1 bag (6 ounces) radishes, thinly sliced

chicken breasts and cook until golden brown, about 5 minutes. Turn chicken over. Reduce heat to medium; cover skillet. Cook chicken until juices run clear when chicken is pierced with tip of knife, 5 to 7 minutes longer. Transfer chicken to cutting board to cool slightly.

5 On very large platter, spread spinach. Top with separate piles of asparagus, green beans, bacon, cucumber, tomatoes, peas, and radishes.

6 When chicken is cool enough to handle, cut into ¾-inch chunks; transfer to platter with vegetables. Cover with plastic wrap and refrigerate until the chicken is completely cold, at least 1 hour and up to 4 hours.

7 Prepare vinaigrette: Into a container with a tight-fitting lid, measure vinegar, oil, maple syrup, mustard, salt, and pepper. Cover and shake until well blended. Refrigerate up to 1 week. Shake well before using. Makes about ¾ cup.

8 Just before serving, drizzle Maple Vinaigrette over salad. Toss salad to evenly coat with vinaigrette.

Maple Vinaigrette

¼ cup cider vinegar or red wine vinegar

¼ cup olive oil

3 tablespoons maple syrup

1 tablespoon plus 1 teaspoon Dijon mustard

½ teaspoon salt

½ teaspoon ground black pepper

EACH SERVING WITHOUT VINAIGRETTE
About 250 calories, 24g protein, 10g carbohydrate, 13g total fat (3g saturated), 4g fiber, 57mg cholesterol, 380mg sodium

EACH TABLESPOON VINAIGRETTE
About 55 calories, 0g protein, 4g carbohydrate, 5g total fat (1g saturated), 0g fiber, 0mg cholesterol, 105mg sodium

POTLUCK PREP Prepare far enough in advance to allow time for proper chilling. For ease of transport in a cooler, arrange salad in a large rectangular Pyrex dish; cover with plastic wrap and set on freezer packs. Or, you could use a deep trifle dish and layer in the ingredients instead, starting with spinach. In either case, keep salad in the cooler until ready to serve, then toss with vinaigrette. Bring serving tongs.

HONEYDEW AND LIME SOUP

TOTAL TIME 10 minutes plus chilling · **MAKES** 6 cups or 6 servings

This flavor-packed cold soup will be an unexpected treat for your fellow picnickers.

1 In blender, pulse melon with lime juice, cilantro, hot sauce, and salt until pureed.

2 Transfer soup to airtight container; cover and refrigerate until chilled, about 2 hours. Stir before serving.

1 honeydew melon (5 pounds), chilled, cut into 1-inch chunks (8 cups)

¼ cup fresh lime juice

¼ cup loosely packed fresh cilantro leaves

1 teaspoon jalapeño hot sauce

⅛ teaspoon salt

EACH SERVING
About 85 calories, 1g protein, 23g carbohydrate, 0g fat, 2g fiber, 0mg cholesterol, 80mg sodium

POTLUCK PREP Prepare soup far enough in advance to allow for proper chilling. Transport chilled soup in chilled thermos bottles to keep it as cold as possible. Bring demitasse cups for serving so fellow potluckers can enjoy their soup sans spoons, if they'd like.

SEAFOOD SALAD

ACTIVE TIME 50 minutes · **TOTAL TIME** 65 minutes plus chilling
MAKES 6 cups or 12 servings

This cold shrimp and squid salad, dressed simply with olive oil and fresh lemon juice, is perfect for a hot summer night.

1   From 1 lemon, grate 1 teaspoon peel and squeeze 2 tablespoons juice. Cut remaining lemon in half and squeeze juice into 4-quart saucepan; add bay leaves. Fill saucepan with *3 inches water;* cover and heat to boiling over high heat. Meanwhile, in large bowl, combine tomatoes, olives, parsley, oil, salt, pepper, and lemon peel and juice.

2   Rinse squid under cold running water. Slice squid bodies crosswise into ½-inch-wide rings. Cut tentacles into several pieces if large.

3   To boiling water in saucepan, add shrimp; cook just until opaque throughout, 1 to 2 minutes. With slotted spoon, transfer shrimp to colander. Add to bowl with tomato mixture.

4   Return water to boiling. Add squid; cook just until opaque, 30 seconds to 1 minute. Drain squid in colander; add to shrimp in bowl. Toss until well combined. Cover and refrigerate at least 1 hour or up to 4 hours.

2 lemons

2 bay leaves

1 pint grape tomatoes

½ cup Gaeta or Niçoise olives, pitted

½ cup loosely packed fresh parsley leaves, chopped

2 tablespoons extra-virgin olive oil

½ teaspoon salt

¼ teaspoon coarsely ground black pepper

1 pound cleaned squid

1 pound medium shrimp, shelled and deveined, with tail part of shell left on if you like

EACH SERVING
About 95 calories, 12g protein, 3g carbohydrate, 4g total fat (1g saturated), 2g fiber, 143mg cholesterol, 230mg sodium

POTLUCK PREP Prepare far enough in advance to allow time for proper chilling. Transport in tightly covered dish set on freezer packs in a cooler. Bring serving spoon or tongs.

FRESH FRUIT WITH RASPBERRY-LIME DIPPING SAUCE

TOTAL TIME 20 minutes · MAKES 2 cups or 8 servings

If Greek yogurt is not available, you can substitute strained regular yogurt: Spoon 2 cups plain low-fat yogurt into a large sieve lined with cheesecloth or a coffee filter set over a bowl; cover and refrigerate 2 hours. Transfer the drained yogurt to a medium bowl; discard the liquid.

1 cup raspberries

1 lime

1½ cups reduced-fat (2%) Greek (strained) yogurt

¼ cup packed light brown sugar

assorted fresh fruit for dipping (such as strawberries, grapes, cut-up melon, banana or kiwifruit slices, and plum, peach, nectarine, pear, and/or apricot wedges)

1   Place raspberries in sieve set over bowl. With back of spoon, mash and press raspberries through sieve into bowl; discard seeds. From lime, grate 1 teaspoon peel and squeeze 1 tablespoon juice.

2   Add lime peel and juice, yogurt, and brown sugar to bowl with raspberry puree and stir to combine. Transfer to airtight container and refrigerate up to 1 day.

3   To serve, spoon sauce into serving bowl and place on large platter. Arrange fruit on same platter.

EACH ¼ CUP SAUCE
About 55 calories, 3g protein, 10g carbohydrate, 1g total fat (1g saturated), 1g fiber, 2mg cholesterol, 15mg sodium

POTLUCK PREP Dipping sauce and fruit can be transported in an insulated bag or picnic basket. Fruit that won't discolor when cut can be prepped in advance: melon and mangoes cut into bite-size chunks, kiwi into slices, plums into wedges. Fruit that will discolor, like bananas, apples, pears, and peaches, can either be cut and then sprinkled with lemon or lime juice or be brought whole to the picnic and sliced right before serving. To keep the fruit juices from bleeding into one another, transport the different cut fruits in separate containers. Bring a platter for serving.

· Fall ·
TAILGATE PARTY

——— MENU ———

Hot Mulled Wine

Warm Spiced Cider

Hot-Pepper Nuts

Easy Spicy Cheese Straws

Jicama and Orange Salad

Garden Macaroni Salad

Grilled Garlic and
Herb Bread

Salsa Verde Enchiladas

Paprika Steak with
Pimiento Salsa

Butterscotch Blondies

Hazelnut Brownies

———————————

Hot Mulled Wine and Warm Spiced Cider provide spiked and non-alcoholic warm-ups, coupled with two crunchy noshes—Hot-Pepper Nuts and homemade cheese straws. For main courses, an enchilada casserole is cooked at home and transported to the tailgate piping hot, while a smoked-paprika-rubbed skirt steak is thrown onto a small portable grill along with some cheesy good Italian bread. We've kept the sides simple with two salads: One features macaroni, the other, jicama. And it's bars for dessert—brownies and blondies—so you can enjoy your sweets in your seats!

HOT MULLED WINE

ACTIVE TIME 10 minutes · **TOTAL TIME** 30 minutes
MAKES 8 generous cups or 16 servings

If you wish, add other whole spices, such as cardamom pods, allspice berries, or even black peppercorns.

1 In nonreactive 4-quart saucepan, combine sugar, water, orange, lemon, cinnamon sticks, and cloves; heat to boiling over high heat until sugar has dissolved, stirring. Reduce heat to medium and cook 3 minutes.

2 Add wine to saucepan and heat until hot (do not boil), stirring.

2 cups sugar

1 cup water

1 small orange, thinly sliced

1 small lemon, thinly sliced

3 cinnamon sticks (3 inches each)

8 whole cloves

1 bottle (750 ml) dry red wine

EACH SERVING
About 170 calories, 0g protein, 28g carbohydrate, 0g fat, 0g fiber, 0mg cholesterol, 5mg sodium

POTLUCK PREP Mull wine right before leaving; strain into thermos bottles. Also bring heatproof cups or mugs.

WARM SPICED CIDER

ACTIVE TIME 10 minutes · **TOTAL TIME** 40 minutes
MAKES 16 cups or 20 servings

Nothing says fall tailgate like apple cider warmed with the comforting flavors of clove and cinnamon.

1 large orange

12 cloves

1 lemon

6 cinnamon sticks (3 inches each)

1 gallon apple cider

EACH SERVING
About 95 calories, 0g protein, 24g carbohydrate, 0g fat, 0g fiber, 0mg cholesterol, 6mg sodium

1 Cut two ½-inch-thick slices from middle of orange. Insert 6 cloves into skin of each orange slice, spacing cloves evenly. Refrigerate remaining orange for another use. With vegetable peeler, from lemon, remove 1-inch-wide continuous strip of peel. Refrigerate lemon for another use.

2 In nonreactive 5-quart saucepot, combine clove-studded orange slices with lemon peel, cinnamon sticks, and apple cider; heat to boiling over high heat. Reduce heat; cover and simmer 15 minutes.

3 Pour hot cider through strainer into thermos.

POTLUCK PREP Prepare right before leaving; strain into thermos bottles. Also bring heatproof cups or mugs.

HOT-PEPPER NUTS

ACTIVE TIME 5 minutes · **TOTAL TIME** 30 minutes · **MAKES** 2 cups or 8 servings

Spiced nuts are a perfect nibble for a tailgate—they're easy to transport and addictively delicious.

8 ounces walnuts (2 cups)

1 tablespoon butter or margarine, melted

2 teaspoons soy sauce

1/2 to 1 teaspoon hot pepper sauce

1 Preheat oven to 350°F. Lightly grease 15" by 10½" jelly-roll pan. Add walnuts and melted butter; toss until coated. Bake walnuts until well toasted, about 25 minutes, stirring occasionally.

2 Drizzle soy sauce and hot pepper sauce over nuts, tossing until well mixed. Cool completely in pan on wire rack. Store nuts in airtight container up to 1 month.

EACH 1/4 CUP
About 211 calories, 4g protein, 6g carbohydrate, 21g total fat (3g saturated), 2g fiber, 4mg cholesterol, 116mg sodium

Sweet-and-Spicy Nuts
Prepare nuts as directed above but substitute **2 tablespoons sugar, 1½ teaspoons Worcestershire sauce, ½ teaspoon ground red pepper (cayenne), and ¼ teaspoon salt** for soy sauce and hot pepper sauce.

Curried Nuts
Prepare nuts as directed above but substitute **2 teaspoons curry powder, ½ teaspoon ground cumin, and ½ teaspoon salt** for soy sauce and hot pepper sauce.

POTLUCK PREP Transport in an airtight container.

EASY SPICY CHEESE STRAWS

ACTIVE TIME 30 minutes · **TOTAL TIME** 1 hour 10 minutes
MAKES 48 cheese straws

You can substitute Parmesan or Asiago for the Cheddar when making these quick and crunchy bites.

1 Preheat oven to 375°F. Grease 2 large cookie sheets. In small bowl, combine paprika, thyme, ground red pepper, and salt.

2 Unfold 1 puff-pastry sheet. On lightly floured surface, with floured rolling pin, roll pastry into 14-inch square. Lightly brush with egg white. Sprinkle half of paprika mixture over pastry. Sprinkle half of Cheddar over half of pastry. Fold pastry over to cover cheese, forming rectangle. With rolling pin, lightly roll over pastry to seal layers together. With pizza wheel or knife, cut pastry crosswise into 1/2-inch-wide strips.

3 Place strips 1/2 inch apart on cookie sheets, twisting each strip twice to form a spiral and pressing ends against cookie sheet to prevent strips from uncurling. Bake cheese straws until golden, 20 to 22 minutes. Transfer to wire racks to cool.

4 Repeat with remaining puff-pastry sheet, egg white, paprika mixture, and cheese. Store in airtight container up to 1 week.

1 tablespoon paprika

1/2 teaspoon dried thyme

1/4 to 1/2 teaspoon ground red pepper (cayenne)

1/4 teaspoon salt

1 package (17 1/4 ounces) frozen puff-pastry sheets, thawed

1 large egg white, lightly beaten

8 ounces sharp Cheddar cheese, shredded (2 cups)

EACH STRAW
About 78 calories, 2g protein, 5g carbohydrate, 5g total fat (2g saturated), 0g fiber, 5mg cholesterol, 68mg sodium

JICAMA AND ORANGE SALAD

TOTAL TIME 45 minutes · **MAKES** 20 side-dish servings

This refreshing salad complements the Tex-Mex entrées on this menu.

1 Using sharp knife, trim top and bottom of jicama and generously peel tough brown skin. Cut jicama into matchstick-size pieces; you should have about 8 cups. Peel cucumber in alternating strips; cut in half lengthwise, then into ¼-inch-thick half-moons.

2 With knife, cut peel and white pith from oranges and discard. Cut each orange crosswise into ¼-inch rounds; cut each round in half and transfer to large bowl. From limes, grate 2 teaspoons peel and squeeze 5 tablespoons juice.

3 To bowl with oranges, add jicama, cucumber, lime peel and juice, cilantro, oil, ground red pepper, and salt. Toss well. Serve immediately or refrigerate up to 4 hours.

1 large jicama (2 pounds)

1 English (seedless) cucumber

4 medium navel oranges (2¼ pounds total)

3 to 4 limes

1 cup packed fresh cilantro leaves, coarsely chopped

1 tablespoon vegetable oil

⅛ teaspoon ground red pepper (cayenne)

¼ teaspoon salt

EACH SERVING
about 40 calories, 1g protein, 8g carbohydrate, 1g total fat (1g saturated), 3g fiber, 0mg cholesterol, 35mg sodium

POTLUCK PREP Transport in a covered container. Serve chilled or at room temperature.

GARDEN MACARONI SALAD

ACTIVE TIME 25 minutes · **TOTAL TIME** 40 minutes
MAKES 8 cups or 12 side-dish servings

This is macaroni salad with a twist—corkscrew pasta instead of elbows and loaded with colorful, crisp vegetables.

1 Heat covered 4-quart saucepan of *salted water* to boiling over high heat. Add pasta and cook as label directs.

2 Meanwhile, from lemon, grate 1 teaspoon peel and squeeze 3 tablespoons juice. Transfer peel and juice to serving bowl; add mayonnaise, milk, salt, and pepper. With wire whisk, stir mayonnaise mixture until smooth.

3 Drain pasta. Rinse with cold running water; drain again.

4 Add pasta, peas, radishes, zucchini, carrot, yellow pepper, and chives to mayonnaise mixture in bowl; toss until evenly mixed. Cover and refrigerate up to 1 day.

8 ounces corkscrew (rotini) pasta

1 large lemon

2/3 cup light mayonnaise

1/3 cup milk

1/2 teaspoon salt

1/2 teaspoon ground black pepper

1 cup frozen peas, thawed

5 radishes, cut into 1/2-inch chunks

1 small zucchini (about 6 ounces), cut into 1/2-inch chunks

1 medium carrot, peeled and shredded

1/2 medium yellow pepper, cut into 1/2-inch pieces

1/4 cup chopped fresh chives

EACH SERVING
About 135 calories, 4g protein, 19g carbohydrate, 5g total fat (1g saturated), 2g fiber, 5mg cholesterol, 245mg sodium

POTLUCK PREP Prepare far enough in advance so it has time to get completely cold in the refrigerator. Transport in a covered container; if weather is warm, carry it in a cooler.

GRILLED GARLIC AND HERB BREAD

ACTIVE TIME 10 minutes · **TOTAL TIME** about 20 minutes
MAKES 6 side-dish servings

Like the spiced nuts on page 103, this is a recipe you can have fun with and bring several flavor selections, if you like.

1 Evenly spread cheese on cut sides of bread. Sprinkle bottom half of bread with tomato. Replace top half of bread. Wrap bread tightly in heavy-duty foil.

2 Prepare outdoor grill for covered direct grilling over medium heat.

3 Place foil-wrapped bread on hot grill rack. Cover grill and cook 10 minutes, turning over once halfway through grilling.

4 Transfer bread to cutting board. To serve, carefully remove foil. With serrated knife, cut bread crosswise into slices.

5 tablespoons soft spreadable cheese with garlic and herbs

½ (16-ounce) long loaf French or Italian bread, split horizontally in half

1 plum tomato, seeded and chopped

EACH SERVING
About 155 calories, 4g protein, 20g carbohydrate, 7g total fat (4g saturated), 1g fiber, 15 mg cholesterol, 305mg sodium

POTLUCK PREP Check with the cook as to the diameter of his or her portable grill. It's possible you might want to cut and wrap the prepped bread in smaller portions so that they will fit on the grill. Also bring a cutting board and serrated bread knife to cut the bread, as well as a basket to hold it.

Basil-Romano Bread

Instead of the soft cheese, brush cut sides of bread with **2 tablespoons bottled Italian salad dressing.** Instead of the tomato, sprinkle bottom half of bread with **⅓ cup torn fresh basil leaves** and **¼ cup freshly grated Pecorino-Romano cheese.** Continue as directed opposite.

EACH SERVING
About 140 calories, 5g protein, 20g carbohydrate, 4g total fat (1g saturated fat), 1g fiber, 4mg cholesterol, 310 mg sodium

Horseradish-Chive Bread

In small bowl, combine **2 tablespoons light mayonnaise, 1 tablespoon bottled white horseradish,** and **1 tablespoon chopped fresh chives.** Spread mayonnaise mixture on cut sides of bread instead of the soft cheese. Omit tomato. Continue as directed opposite.

EACH SERVING
About 120 calories, 3g protein, 21g carbohydrate, 2g total fat (1g saturated), 1g fiber, 2 mg cholesterol, 265mg sodium

SALSA VERDE ENCHILADAS

ACTIVE TIME 50 minutes · **TOTAL TIME** 1 hour 10 minutes
MAKES 2 casseroles, 4 main-dish servings each

This dish will warm and satisfy your guests. If two casseroles are more than you need, freeze one to enjoy another day.

1 Remove meat from chickens and coarsely shred; place in medium bowl (you will need 5½ cups; reserve any extra for use another day). Discard skin and bones. Stir ½ cup salsa verde into chicken to evenly coat.

2 Preheat oven to 350°F. Grease two 13" by 9" baking dishes; set aside.

3 In 12-inch skillet, heat remaining salsa verde, green onions, and lime juice to boiling over medium-high heat. Boil 2 minutes, stirring occasionally. Stir in 2 tablespoons cilantro; keep warm over very low heat.

4 With tongs, place 1 tortilla in salsa verde mixture; heat 10 seconds. Place tortilla on waxed paper; top with about ⅓ cup shredded-chicken mixture. Roll up tortilla and place, seam side down, in prepared baking dish. Repeat with remaining tortillas and chicken mixture, arranging 8 tortillas in each dish.

2 rotisserie chickens

2 jars (16 to 17.6 ounces each) mild salsa verde

6 green onions, thinly sliced

¼ cup fresh lime juice (from 2 to 3 limes)

½ cup loosely packed fresh cilantro leaves, chopped

16 (6-inch) corn tortillas

1 container (8 ounces) reduced-fat sour cream

½ cup reduced-sodium chicken broth

1 package (8 ounces) reduced-fat (2%) shredded Mexican cheese blend (2 cups)

POTLUCK PREP Bake both casseroles right before leaving. Cover with foil and transport in an insulated food carrier. Bring a server.

5 Stir sour cream and broth into remaining salsa verde mixture in skillet; spoon over filled tortillas. Cover the dishes with foil and bake 15 minutes. Remove foil; sprinkle each dish with 1 cup cheese and 1 tablespoon cilantro. Bake until cheese melts, about 5 minutes longer.

EACH SERVING
About 465 calories, 39g protein, 36g carbohydrate, 18g total fat (7g saturated), 3g fiber, 117mg cholesterol, 785mg sodium

PAPRIKA STEAK WITH PIMIENTO SALSA

ACTIVE TIME 10 minutes · **TOTAL TIME** 20 minutes
MAKES 6 main-dish servings

Smoked paprika (*pimentón de La Vera*) has a distinct and delicious flavor. It's increasingly available in larger supermarkets and is worth searching out.

1 Rub steak all over with paprika. Sprinkle both sides with salt. Place in zip-tight plastic bag in refrigerator until ready to grill.

2 In small airtight container, combine pimientos, garlic, almonds, raisins, capers, oil, and vinegar. Refrigerate until ready to cook. Makes about ¾ cup salsa.

3 Prepare outdoor grill for direct grilling over medium heat.

4 Place steak on hot grill rack. Cook steak 6 to 8 minutes for medium-rare or until desired doneness, turning over once. Transfer steak to cutting board; let stand 5 minutes for easier slicing. Thinly slice steak against the grain. Serve with salsa.

1½ pounds beef skirt steak

1 tablespoon mild smoked Spanish paprika or regular paprika

1 teaspoon salt

1 jar (4 ounces) sliced pimientos, drained

1 small garlic clove, crushed with garlic press

¼ cup blanched almonds, coarsely chopped

2 tablespoons raisins, coarsely chopped

1 tablespoon capers, drained and chopped

1 tablespoon olive oil

1 tablespoon red wine vinegar

EACH SERVING STEAK
About 190 calories, 27g protein, 1g carbohydrate, 8g total fat (3g saturated), 0g fiber, 81mg cholesterol, 440mg sodium

EACH TABLESPOON SALSA
About 30 calories, 1g protein, 2g carbohydrate, 2g total fat (0g saturated), 1g fiber, 0mg cholesterol, 25 mg sodium

POTLUCK PREP Transport prepped steak, ready for the grill, and salsa in a cooler. (You might want to double bag the steak to avoid any leakage.) Bring a cutting board and chef's knife to cut the steak, and a serving platter and tongs.

BUTTERSCOTCH BLONDIES

ACTIVE TIME 15 minutes · **TOTAL TIME** 35 to 40 minutes · **MAKES** 24 blondies

Perfect for a tailgate, these bars are also a great choice for any type of potluck.

1 Preheat oven to 350°F. Grease 13" by 9" baking pan.

2 On waxed paper, combine flour, baking powder, and salt.

3 In 3-quart saucepan, melt butter over medium heat. Remove saucepan from heat; stir in brown sugar and vanilla. Add eggs; stir until well mixed. Stir in flour mixture and pecans just until blended. Spread batter in prepared baking pan.

4 Bake until toothpick inserted 2 inches from edge comes out almost clean, 20 to 25 minutes. Do not overbake; blondies will firm up as they cool. Cool in pan on wire rack.

5 When cool, cut lengthwise into 4 strips, then cut each strip crosswise into 6 pieces.

1 cup all-purpose flour

2 teaspoons baking powder

¾ teaspoon salt

6 tablespoons butter or margarine

1¾ cups packed light brown sugar

2 teaspoons vanilla extract

2 large eggs, lightly beaten

1 cup pecans, coarsely chopped

EACH BLONDIE
About 145 calories, 0g protein, 20g carbohydrate, 7g total fat (2g saturated), 1g fiber, 26mg cholesterol, 150mg sodium

POTLUCK PREP Transport in a cookie tin.

HAZELNUT BROWNIES

ACTIVE TIME 30 minutes · **TOTAL TIME** 55 to 60 minutes · **MAKES** 24 brownies

Chocolate-hazelnut spread and toasted hazelnuts offer a double dose of nutty goodness.

1 Preheat oven to 350°F. Grease 13" by 9" baking pan.

2 In 3-quart saucepan, heat butter, unsweetened chocolate, and semisweet chocolate over medium-low heat until melted, stirring frequently. Remove saucepan from heat; stir in hazelnut spread.

3 Add sugar and vanilla, stirring until well blended. Add eggs; stir until well mixed. Stir in flour, hazelnuts, and salt just until blended. Spread batter in prepared baking pan.

4 Bake until toothpick inserted 2 inches from edge comes out almost clean, 25 to 30 minutes. Cool in pan on wire rack.

5 When cool, cut brownies lengthwise into 4 strips, then cut each strip crosswise into 6 pieces.

¾ cup butter or margarine (1½ sticks)

4 ounces unsweetened chocolate

2 ounces semisweet chocolate

½ cup (about half 13-ounce jar) chocolate-hazelnut spread

1½ cups sugar

1 teaspoon vanilla extract

4 large eggs, lightly beaten

1 cup all-purpose flour

1 cup hazelnuts (filberts), toasted and coarsely chopped (see Tip)

½ teaspoon salt

EACH BROWNIE
About 230 calories, 4g protein, 23g carbohydrate, 15g total fat (6g saturated), 2g fiber, 52mg cholesterol, 125mg sodium

TIP Unless you buy hazelnuts that have already had their skins removed, you'll need to do that after you toast them, as the skins taste bitter. To toast, place the nuts in a single layer in a metal baking pan in a preheated 350°F oven. Baked until portions of the nuts without skin are light brown, about fifteen minutes, shaking or stirring the nuts occasionally. Wrap the hot nuts in a clean towel. With your hands, roll them back and forth to remove most of the skin.

POTLUCK PREP Transport in a cookie tin.

· Day After ·
Thanksgiving
DINNER PARTY

Cranberry Mojitos

Cranberry-Almond Salad

Cranberry-Fig Conserve
with Brie

Garlic and Thyme
Green Beans

Maple-Roasted Squash

Turkey Escarole Soup

Turkey and Veggie
Lasagna

Turkey and Mashed
Potato "Pie"

Pumpkin Cheesecake
Crème Caramel

You've survived the stress and strain of turkey day. Now it's time to kick off your shoes, invite your friends over, and start a new holiday tradition at your house. This get-together is all about ease of preparation. Three potluckers will prepare recipes based on leftover turkey. The rest of the dishes can be leftovers from everyone's Thanksgiving feast, but just in case your friends have been wiped clean, we've provided a selection of recipes in keeping with the day-after-Thanksgiving theme.

CRANBERRY MOJITOS

TOTAL TIME 10 minutes · **MAKES** 10 cups or 20 servings

This delicious pitcher drink declares this pot-luck is a party!

1 From limes, grate 1 tablespoon peel and squeeze ½ cup juice. In blender container, combine peel and juice, mint leaves, and sugar. Cover blender and pulse until mint is chopped.

2 Into large pitcher, pour mint mixture, cranberry juice, and rum. Stir in club soda.

3 To serve, add ice to pitcher or pour over ice in glasses. Garnish with mint sprigs.

4 to 5 limes

3 cups loosely packed fresh mint leaves

½ cup sugar

1 bottle (32 ounces) cranberry-juice cocktail

2 cups golden or light rum

3 cups club soda or seltzer, chilled

8 cups ice cubes

mint sprigs for garnish

EACH SERVING
About 90 calories, 0g protein, 12g carbohydrate, 0g fat, 1g fiber, 0mg cholesterol, 10 mg sodium

POTLUCK PREP Mix these mojitos, minus the club soda, and transport in a covered pitcher, along with a zip-tight plastic bag of mint sprigs. When you arrive at the party, add the club soda, then pour over ice, garnish, and serve.

CRANBERRY-ALMOND SALAD

TOTAL TIME 5 minutes · **MAKES** 16 cups or 8 servings

Around the holidays, some supermarkets sell a salad mix with spinach, almonds, and cranberries, which we use here. If you can't find it in your area, substitute 3 bags (5 to 6 ounces each) baby spinach, 1/3 cup sliced almonds, and 1/3 cup dried cranberries.

1   In small bowl, whisk oil, vinegar, mustard, salt, and pepper until blended. Cover and refrigerate until ready to serve.

2   In large serving bowl, toss spinach, almonds, and cranberries with dressing; sprinkle with blue cheese.

3 tablespoons walnut oil

2 tablespoons white wine vinegar

1/2 teaspoon Dijon mustard

1/4 teaspoon salt

1/8 teaspoon coarsely ground black pepper

3 bags (5½ ounces each) baby spinach salad with almonds and cranberries

1/2 cup crumbled blue cheese

EACH SERVING
About 65 calories, 2g protein, 3g carbohydrate, 5g total fat (1g saturated), 3g fiber, 3mg cholesterol, 130mg sodium

POTLUCK PREP Prepare dressing and store in a tightly closed jar. In advance, crumble blue cheese and measure out the almonds and cranberries if necessary; store separately. Carry salad ingredients to the potluck in the salad bowl you intend to use; remember to take salad tongs. Toss salad together right before serving.

CRANBERRY-FIG CONSERVE WITH BRIE

ACTIVE TIME 10 minutes · **TOTAL TIME** 15 minutes plus chilling
MAKES 24 appetizer servings

What an easy, elegant way to start off your dinner. Allowing the Brie to soften at room temperature enhances the flavor of the cheese.

1 In 2-quart saucepan, heat brown sugar, brandy, and water to boiling over high heat; boil 2 minutes. From lemon, grate 1 teaspoon peel and squeeze 2 tablespoons juice.

2 Add cranberries, figs, jalapeño, and lemon peel and juice to saucepan; heat to boiling, stirring frequently. Reduce heat to medium; cook until most cranberries pop and mixture thickens slightly, about 5 minutes. Cover and refrigerate at least 3 hours or up to 1 week. Makes about 3 cups.

3 About 1 hour before serving, remove Brie and conserve from refrigerator; let stand at room temperature to warm slightly.

4 To serve, spoon some conserve over Brie if you like; serve with bread, if using, and remaining conserve in small serving bowl.

2/3 cup packed brown sugar

1/4 cup brandy

2/3 cup water

1 lemon

1 bag (12 ounces) cranberries (3 cups), picked over

8 ounces dried figs, trimmed and each cut into 8 pieces

1 jalapeño chile, chopped

1 wheel (6 to 7 inches in diameter) ripe Brie cheese or one 1-pound wedge

1 loaf French bread, sliced (optional)

EACH SERVING WITHOUT BREAD
About 120 calories, 4g protein, 14g carbohydrate, 5g total fat (3g saturated), 2g fiber, 19mg cholesterol, 120mg sodium

POTLUCK PREP Prepare the conserve so it has enough time to set in the refrigerator. Take it and the Brie out of the refrigerator about an hour before leaving for the potluck so they have a chance to warm to room temperature. Cut the bread right before leaving and transport in a zip-tight plastic bag so the slices don't dry out. Bring a small decorative bowl and spoon for the conserve, a plate large enough to accommodate the Brie, conserve, and bread slices, and a serving knife for the cheese.

GARLIC AND THYME GREEN BEANS

ACTIVE TIME 10 minutes · **TOTAL TIME** 20 minutes · **MAKES** 8 side-dish servings

Because this dish is finished stovetop right before serving, we recommend that the host prepare it.

1 In 12-inch skillet, heat *1 inch water* and ½ teaspoon salt to boiling over high heat. Add green beans; heat to boiling. Reduce heat to low; simmer until tender-crisp, 5 to 10 minutes, depending on thickness of beans; drain. Wipe skillet dry.

2 In same skillet, heat oil and garlic 1 minute over medium heat. Add green beans and cook until hot, about 2 minutes. Remove skillet from heat and toss green beans with thyme, remaining ¼ teaspoon salt, and pepper.

¾ teaspoon salt

2 pounds green beans, trimmed

1 tablespoon olive oil

2 garlic cloves, crushed with garlic press

1 teaspoon fresh thyme leaves

¼ teaspoon ground black pepper

EACH SERVING
About 45 calories, 2g protein, 7g carbohydrate, 2g total fat (0g saturated), 3g fiber, 0mg cholesterol, 100mg sodium

POTLUCK PREP You can cook the green beans to tender-crisp in boiling water earlier in the day; refrigerate in a zip-tight plastic bag until ready to finish.

MAPLE-ROASTED SQUASH

ACTIVE TIME 5 minutes · **TOTAL TIME** 30 minutes · **MAKES** 8 side-dish servings

In the vegetable department, nothing says "fall" like butternut squash. Tossed with a mix of maple syrup and spices that gives it a hint of heat and smoke flavor, it's roasted, which concentrates its own natural sweetness.

1 Preheat oven to 425°F. Line 15½" by 10½" jelly-roll pan with foil. Place squash in pan; drizzle with oil, sprinkle with salt, and toss to combine. Roast squash 15 minutes.

2 Meanwhile, in 1-cup liquid measuring cup, stir maple syrup with pumpkin-pie spice and ground red pepper.

3 Toss squash with maple syrup mixture. Roast until fork-tender, 15 to 20 minutes longer. Spoon squash, along with any pan juices, into serving dish.

1 package (2 pounds) peeled and cubed butternut squash

1 tablespoon olive oil

¼ teaspoon salt

⅓ cup maple syrup

½ teaspoon pumpkin-pie spice

pinch ground red pepper (cayenne)

EACH SERVING
About 100 calories, 1g protein, 22g carbohydrate, 2g total fat (0g saturated), 2g fiber, 0mg cholesterol, 80mg sodium

POTLUCK PREP Roast the squash right before leaving, transfer to a covered serving dish, and transport in an insulated food carrier.

TURKEY ESCAROLE SOUP

ACTIVE TIME 15 minutes · **TOTAL TIME** 25 minutes
MAKES 10 cups or 5 main-dish servings

You can serve this to start the meal or set it out with all the other potluck offerings.

1 In 6-quart Dutch oven, heat oil over medium-high heat until hot. Add carrots, onion, and garlic; cook until onion softens, about 4 minutes, stirring frequently. Stir in broth and water; heat to boiling. Stir in escarole and orzo; heat to boiling.

2 Reduce heat to medium-low; simmer until escarole and orzo are tender, about 6 minutes. Stir in turkey and pepper. Reduce heat to low; simmer until turkey is heated through, about 3 minutes. Serve with Parmesan.

1 tablespoon olive oil

2 cups shredded or matchstick carrots (about two-thirds of a 10-ounce bag)

1 small onion, finely chopped

2 cloves garlic, minced

3 cans (14½ ounces each) chicken broth (5¼ cups)

2 cups water

2 heads escarole (1½ pounds), cut into 1-inch pieces

½ cup orzo pasta

2 cups chopped leftover cooked turkey (10 ounces)

⅛ teaspoon coarsely ground black pepper

½ cup freshly grated Parmesan cheese

EACH SERVING
About 285 calories, 28g protein, 25g carbohydrate, 9g total fat (3g saturated), 6g fiber, 49mg cholesterol, 890mg sodium

POTLUCK PREP Prepare or reheat this right before you leave. Transport it in the soup pot you prepared it in or transfer it to a slow cooker. In either case, be sure to secure the lid. Once at the potluck, if need be, you can set the pot on the stove for a quick simmer, or set the slow cooker on the Keep Warm setting. Bring a serving ladle.

TURKEY AND VEGGIE LASAGNA

ACTIVE TIME 25 minutes · **TOTAL TIME** 1 hour 10 minutes
MAKES 6 main-dish servings

Leftover turkey never had it so good in this hearty, satisfying take on lasagna.

1 In 12-inch nonstick skillet, melt 1 tablespoon butter over medium heat. Add mushrooms, onion, and garlic, and cook until mushrooms are lightly browned, about 8 minutes, stirring occasionally. Set aside.

2 Meanwhile, in 4-quart saucepan, melt remaining 3 tablespoons butter over medium heat. Whisk in flour and cook 1 minute. Gradually whisk in milk and broth until well blended; cook until sauce thickens and boils, stirring frequently. Boil 2 minutes. Set sauce aside.

3 Preheat oven to 375°F. Spray 8-inch glass or ceramic baking dish with nonstick cooking spray. Pour ½ cup sauce in bottom of baking dish; arrange 2 noodles over sauce, overlapping to fit. Top evenly with half of spinach, half of turkey, then ½ cup sauce; sprinkle with ¼ cup Parmesan. Top with 2 noodles, mushroom mixture, ¾ cup mozzarella, then ½ cup sauce. Top with 2 noodles, remaining spinach and turkey, then ¾ cup sauce, and ¼ cup Parmesan. Arrange

4 tablespoons butter or margarine

1 package (10 ounces) sliced mushrooms

1 small onion, finely chopped

1 garlic clove, crushed with garlic press

⅓ cup all-purpose flour

2 cups low-fat (1%) milk, warmed

1 can (14½ ounces) chicken broth (1¾ cups)

8 no-boil lasagna noodles

1 package (10 ounces) frozen chopped spinach, thawed and squeezed dry

2 cups ½-inch pieces leftover cooked turkey (10 ounces)

¾ cup freshly grated Parmesan cheese

1 cup shredded part-skim mozzarella cheese (4 ounces)

remaining noodles on top; spoon remaining sauce over noodles to cover. Sprinkle with remaining mozzarella and Parmesan.

4 Spray sheet of foil with cooking spray (or use nonstick foil); cover baking dish, sprayed (or nonstick) side down. Bake lasagna 30 minutes. Remove foil and bake until hot and bubbly in the center and lightly browned on top, about 15 minutes longer. Let stand 15 minutes for easier serving.

POTLUCK PREP Bake right before leaving and transport to the potluck in an insulated food carrier. Or, if your host prefers, bake for 30 minutes, then take to the potluck and finish browning there.

EACH SERVING
About 445 calories, 33g protein, 36g carbohydrate, 18g total fat (7g saturated), 3g fiber, 57mg cholesterol, 740mg sodium

TURKEY AND MASHED POTATO "PIE"

ACTIVE TIME 10 minutes · **TOTAL TIME** 35 minutes · **MAKES** 6 main dish servings

Leftover mashed potatoes can get stiff when refrigerated, making them hard to spread. If that happens, add a few tablespoons of hot milk and stir until they loosen up.

1 Preheat oven to 375°F. Lightly grease shallow 2-quart glass or ceramic baking dish; set aside.

2 In 3-quart saucepan, melt butter over medium heat. Whisk in flour until smooth; cook 1 minute. Whisk in broth and Worcestershire until well blended; heat to boiling over high heat. Reduce heat to low; simmer 5 minutes, stirring frequently. Stir in turkey and chopped vegetables.

3 Spoon stuffing evenly into bottom of prepared baking dish. Top with turkey mixture. Using back of spoon, evenly spread mashed potatoes over top; sprinkle with Cheddar.

4 Bake casserole until hot and bubbly and cheese begins to brown at edges, about 25 minutes. Let stand 5 minutes for easier serving.

2 tablespoons butter or margarine

2 tablespoons all-purpose flour

1 can (14½ ounces) chicken broth (1¾ cups)

1 teaspoon Worcestershire sauce

2 cups ½-inch pieces leftover cooked turkey (10 ounces)

2 cups leftover cooked vegetables, coarsely chopped

1½ cups leftover stuffing

2 cups leftover mashed potatoes

½ cup shredded sharp Cheddar cheese

EACH SERVING
About 340 calories, 22g protein, 33g carbohydrate, 14g total fat (4g saturated), 4g fiber, 47mg cholesterol, 830mg sodium

POTLUCK PREP Bake right before leaving and transport in an insulated food carrier.

PUMPKIN CHEESECAKE CRÈME CARAMEL

ACTIVE TIME 30 minutes · **TOTAL TIME** 1 hour 40 minutes plus chilling
MAKES 12 servings

Because of all the caramel sauce, be sure to use a deep rectangular platter for serving this delicious, silky smooth dessert.

1 Preheat oven to 350°F. Fill kettle or covered 4-quart saucepan with *water*; heat to boiling over high heat.

2 Meanwhile, from orange, with vegetable peeler, remove 6 strips peel, about 3" by 1" each. With knife, trim off as much white pith as possible from peel. In 1-quart saucepan, heat orange peel, ¾ cup sugar, and ¼ cup water to boiling over medium heat; cover and cook 5 minutes. Remove cover and cook until sugar mixture is amber in color, 1 to 2 minutes longer. Pour hot caramel into 9" by 5" metal loaf pan. With fork, remove and discard orange peel. (Hold loaf pan with potholders to protect hands from heat of caramel.) Set pan aside.

3 In large bowl, with mixer on medium speed, beat cream cheese and remaining ½ cup sugar 2 minutes, occasionally scraping down bowl with rubber spatula. Beat in pumpkin, then eggs, 1 at a time. Reduce mixer speed to low; beat in evaporated milk,

1 orange

1¼ cups sugar

¼ cup water

1 package (8 ounces) cream cheese, softened

1 cup solid pack pumpkin (not pumpkin-pie mix)

6 large eggs

1 can (12 ounces) evaporated milk

½ cup heavy or whipping cream

¼ cup orange-flavor liqueur such as Grand Marnier or triple sec

1 teaspoon vanilla extract

1 teaspoon ground cinnamon

pinch ground nutmeg

pinch salt

cream, liqueur, vanilla, cinnamon, nutmeg, and salt just until well mixed.

EACH SERVING
About 280 calories, 7g protein, 28g carbohydrate, 15g total fat (9g saturated), 1g fiber, 150mg cholesterol, 135mg sodium

4 Pour pumpkin mixture through medium-mesh sieve over caramel in loaf pan, pressing it through with rubber spatula. Place loaf pan in 13" by 9" baking pan; place in oven. Carefully pour *boiling water* into baking pan to come three-quarters up sides of loaf pan.

5 Bake until knife inserted 1 inch from edge of custard comes out clean (center will jiggle), about 1 hour and 10 to 15 minutes. Remove loaf pan from baking pan to cool on wire rack 1 hour. Cover and refrigerate crème caramel at least 8 hours or overnight.

6 To unmold, run small metal spatula or knife around sides of loaf pan; invert crème caramel onto serving plate. Leave loaf pan in place several minutes, allowing caramel syrup to drip from pan onto loaf. (Don't worry if some caramel remains in loaf pan.)

POTLUCK PREP **Prepare earlier in the day or the day before to allow proper chilling time. Transport in loaf pan along with serving dish. At potluck, unmold as directed in step 6.**

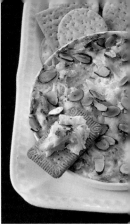

· New Year's Eve ·
POTLUCK PARTY

---- MENU ----

Holiday Champagne Punch   Glazed Ham with Apricots

Hot Crabmeat Spread   Corn Pudding

Spinach and Mandarin   Brussels Sprouts with Garlic
Orange Salad   Butter and Almonds

Cranberry Trifle

————————————•————————————

Potluck is a great way to handle New Year's. Asking friends to bring a dish to come celebrate one last time before years' end makes it a work- and stress-free get-together for everyone. For this menu, we combined elements of indulgence and comfort. Start out with a festive champagne punch served with a hot crabmeat dip, then move on to a dinner that will warm the coldest winter night—a deliciously glazed ham accompanied by smooth and satisfying corn pudding, sautéed Brussels sprouts, and a spinach and orange salad. The grand finale is a showstopper trifle layered with cranberries.

HOLIDAY CHAMPAGNE PUNCH

TOTAL TIME 20 minutes plus freezing · **MAKES** 10 cups or 20 servings

This pretty punch is a sparkling spectacle, its fruit garnish frozen into an icy ring that also helps to keep everything cold.

1 Fill 5-cup ring mold with *½ inch cold water*; freeze until hard, about 45 minutes. Reserve 8 strawberries; hull and slice remaining strawberries. On top of ice in ring mold, decoratively arrange half of sliced strawberries and ½ cup stemmed grapes. Add just enough water to prevent fruit from floating. Freeze until hard, about 45 minutes. Repeat with remaining strawberry slices, another ½ cup stemmed grapes, and enough *water* to cover fruit; freeze until hard, about 45 minutes.

2 With kitchen shears, cut remaining grape stems into small bunches of grapes; arrange grape bunches and reserved whole strawberries alternately in ring mold. Add enough *water* to come up to rim of mold, allowing some fruit to be exposed above water; freeze until hard, about 45 minutes or up to 6 hours.

1 pint strawberries

1 pound seedless green grapes, on stems

2 cups orange juice

¼ cup orange-flavor liqueur such as Grand Marnier or Triple Sec

1 bottle (1 liter) ginger ale, chilled

1 bottle (750 milliliters) champagne or sparkling white wine, chilled

1 bunch fresh mint

POTLUCK PREP To prevent messy sloshing mishaps in transit, pack the ice ring and liquids (still in their original bottles or cartons) in a cooler. Assemble punch at the party.

3 About 15 minutes before serving, in 5-quart punch bowl or bowl large enough to hold ice ring, combine orange juice and orange liqueur. Stir in ginger ale and champagne.

4 Unmold ice ring and turn fruit side up. Tuck small mint sprigs between grapes and strawberries. Add ice ring to punch bowl and serve.

EACH SERVING
About 85 calories, 0g protein,
14g carbohydrate, 0g fat,
1g fiber, 0mg cholesterol,
7mg sodium

This punch features a ring of ice containing artfully arranged strawberries and grapes.

The ring is created by freezing progressive layers of water and fruit. After the ring is frozen solid, you will unmold it and turn it right side up in the punch bowl.

HOT CRABMEAT SPREAD

ACTIVE TIME 10 minutes · **TOTAL TIME** 35 minutes · **MAKES** 12 appetizer servings

This addictive spread has the added crunch of toasted almonds with a little bit of horseradish bite.

1 Preheat oven to 375°F. Spread almonds in 8-inch baking pan. Bake until lightly toasted, 2 to 3 minutes. Pick through crabmeat to remove any pieces of shell, making sure not to break up meat.

2 In medium bowl, stir cream cheese, onion, milk, horseradish, salt, and pepper until blended. Gently stir in crabmeat. Spread mixture into shallow 9-inch baking dish.

3 Sprinkle almonds over crabmeat mixture. Bake until edges brown and center begins to bubble, 20 to 25 minutes. Serve hot with crackers.

3 tablespoons sliced almonds

1 container (8 ounces) lump crabmeat

1 package (8 ounces) cream cheese, softened

3 tablespoons minced onion

1 tablespoon milk

½ teaspoon bottled white horseradish

¼ teaspoon salt

⅛ teaspoon coarsely ground black pepper

assorted crackers

EACH SERVING
About 40 calories, 2g protein, 1g carbohydrate, 3g total fat (2g saturated), 2g fiber, 17mg cholesterol, 70mg sodium

POTLUCK PREP Bake right before leaving. Cover tightly with foil and transport in an insulated food carrier. You could also keep this warm on the buffet table in a mini slow cooker. Bring a box of crackers and a basket or plate to arrange them on.

SPINACH AND MANDARIN ORANGE SALAD

TOTAL TIME 5 minutes · **MAKES** 8 first-course servings

Just five ingredients but what an incredible combination of flavors and textures—the tender green goodness of baby spinach, the juicy sweetness of mandarin oranges, and the crunchy rich flavor of honey-roasted almonds.

Place spinach in large salad bowl. Drizzle poppy-seed dressing on top; squeeze juice from lemon half over salad. Just before serving, toss to combine; top with mandarin-orange sections and sliced almonds.

2 bags (5 to 6 ounces each) baby spinach

1/3 cup bottled poppy-seed salad dressing

1/2 lemon

1 can (11 ounces) mandarin-orange sections, drained and patted dry

1/2 cup honey-roasted sliced almonds (half 3¾-ounce bag)

EACH SERVING
About 95 calories, 3g protein, 6g carbohydrate, 7g total fat (1g saturated), 5g fiber, 0mg cholesterol, 125mg sodium

POTLUCK PREP Wash and spin dry spinach if necessary. Transport in zip-tight plastic bags set in the salad bowl you intend to use, along with the bottle of salad dressing, lemon, can of orange sections, almonds measured into a small zip-tight plastic bag or container, and salad tongs. Put salad together as directed above before serving.

GLAZED HAM WITH APRICOTS

ACTIVE TIME 35 minutes · **TOTAL TIME** 2 hours 45 minutes
MAKES 16 main-dish servings

Ham halves are available as butt or shank. The shank half looks more like a classic whole ham because it contains the leg bone. It's also easier to carve than the butt half, and less fatty, too.

1 fully cooked bone-in smoked half ham (7 pounds)

1 package (6 ounces) dried apricot halves

2 tablespoons whole cloves

1/2 cup orange marmalade or apricot jam

2 tablespoons grainy country-style Dijon mustard

EACH SERVING
About 240 calories, 29g protein, 16g carbohydrate, 7g total fat (2g saturated), 0g fiber, 62mg cholesterol, 1,525mg sodium

1 Preheat oven to 325°F. With knife, remove skin and trim all but 1/8 inch fat from ham. Secure apricots with cloves to fat side of ham in rows, leaving some space between apricots. Place ham, fat side up, on rack in large roasting pan (17" by 11½"); add *1 cup water*. Cover pan tightly with foil. Bake 2 hours.

2 After ham has baked 1 hour 45 minutes, prepare glaze: In 1-quart saucepan, heat marmalade and mustard to boiling over medium-high heat. Remove foil from ham and carefully brush with some glaze.

3 Continue to bake ham 30 to 40 minutes longer, brushing with glaze every 15 minutes, until instant-read meat thermometer inserted away from the bone reaches 135°F. Internal temperature of ham will rise 5° to 10°F upon standing. (Some apricots may fall off into pan as you glaze.)

4 Transfer ham to cutting board; cover and let stand 20 minutes for easier slicing. Slice ham and serve with apricots from pan.

POTLUCK PREP Bake the ham right before leaving. Remove it from the oven and wrap it with foil; transport it in the roasting pan along with a serving platter. Slice ham at potluck right before serving (so everyone can first admire your beautifully glazed ham), arranging the slices and apricots on the platter. It might also be fun to bring a selection of different mustards for people to choose from.

CORN PUDDING

ACTIVE TIME 15 minutes · **TOTAL TIME** 1 hour · **MAKES** 12 side-dish servings

Corn pudding is a tasty alternative to potatoes. In this version, you get a triple dose of corn goodness—cream-style corn, corn kernels, and cornmeal.

1 Preheat oven to 350°F. Grease 13" by 9" baking dish; set aside.

2 In large bowl, combine cream-style corn, fresh or frozen corn kernels, sour cream, cornmeal, egg yolks, salt, and pepper.

3 In small bowl, with mixer on high speed, beat egg whites until stiff peaks form. Fold whites into corn mixture; pour into prepared baking dish.

4 Bake pudding until edges are set and center jiggles slightly, about 45 minutes. Let pudding stand on wire rack 10 minutes to set before serving.

1 can (14¾ ounces) cream-style corn

3 cups fresh corn kernels (from about 6 ears) or 1 bag (16 ounces) frozen corn

1 container (16 ounces) sour cream

¾ cup cornmeal

3 large eggs, separated

½ teaspoon salt

½ teaspoon coarsely ground black pepper

EACH SERVING
About 200 calories, 6g protein, 25g carbohydrate, 10g total fat (5g saturated), 2g fiber, 70mg cholesterol, 330mg sodium

POTLUCK PREP Bake right before leaving. Allow to set for 10 minutes, then cover tightly with foil and transport in an insulated food carrier.

BRUSSELS SPROUTS WITH GARLIC BUTTER AND ALMONDS

ACTIVE TIME 20 minutes · **TOTAL TIME** 35 minutes
MAKES 5 cups or 12 side-dish servings

The secret to Brussels sprouts is not to over-cook them, otherwise you end up with sprouts that taste—and smell—cabbagey. Treat Brussels sprouts right and you'll be rewarded with great texture and a fabulous nutty flavor that's enhanced in this recipe by the addition of toasted almonds.

1 In nonstick 12-inch skillet, cook almonds over medium heat until browned, 4 to 5 minutes, stirring frequently. Transfer almonds to cup; set aside.

2 In same skillet, melt butter over medium heat. Stir in garlic, Brussels sprouts, water, and salt; cover and cook until sprouts are just tender, 10 to 12 minutes, stirring occasionally. (You may need to stir Brussels sprouts mixture more frequently during final minutes of cooking to avoid overbrowning the garlic.)

3 Transfer Brussels sprouts to serving bowl; sprinkle with almonds to serve.

½ cup slivered almonds

2 tablespoons butter or margarine

4 large garlic cloves, slivered

3 containers (10 ounces each) Brussels sprouts, trimmed and each cut lengthwise into quarters

⅓ cup water

1 teaspoon salt

EACH SERVING
About 80 calories, 3g protein, 7g carbohydrate, 5g total fat (2g saturated), 3g fiber, 5mg cholesterol, 230mg sodium

POTLUCK PREP Because this is a last-minute preparation, we recommend that the host make it.

CRANBERRY TRIFLE

TOTAL TIME 50 minutes plus chilling · **MAKES** 12 servings

This layered dessert is a spectacular way to end the meal and welcome in the New Year!

1 From oranges, grate 1 teaspoon peel and place in 4-quart saucepan. With knife, remove all remaining peel and white pith from oranges. Holding 1 orange at a time over same saucepan, to catch juice, cut sections from between membranes and add to saucepan, then squeeze juice from membranes into saucepan; discard membranes.

2 Set aside a few cranberries for garnish. In same saucepan, stir remaining cranberries with water, sugar, ginger, cinnamon, and allspice. Heat to boiling over high heat, stirring often. Reduce heat to medium; cook until cranberries pop and sauce thickens slightly, 15 to 17 minutes, stirring occasionally. Remove from heat; cool to room temperature.

3 Meanwhile, in medium bowl, with mixer on medium speed, beat cream until soft peaks form. In large bowl, with wire whisk, prepare pudding with milk as label directs. Immediately fold whipped cream into pudding until blended.

4 In 3-quart glass trifle bowl or other serving bowl, place one-third of cake cubes.

2 navel oranges

1 bag (12 ounces) fresh cranberries (about 3 cups)

1¼ cups water

1 cup sugar

2 tablespoons chopped crystallized ginger

¼ teaspoon ground cinnamon

⅛ teaspoon ground allspice

1 cup heavy or whipping cream

1 package (4 servings) vanilla-flavored instant pudding and pie filling

2 cups milk

1 frozen pound cake (16 ounces), cut into ¾-inch cubes

Spoon one-third of cranberry mixture (about 1 cup) over cake, spreading to side of bowl. Top with one-third of pudding (about 1¼ cups). Repeat layering two more times. Garnish with reserved cranberries.

5 Cover trifle and refrigerate at least 4 hours or up to 2 days.

EACH SERVING
About 375 calories, 4g protein, 53g carbohydrate, 17g total fat (10g saturated), 2g fiber, 75mg cholesterol, 285mg sodium

POTLUCK PREP Prepare in the morning or the day before to allow time for it to chill properly. Cover tightly with plastic. If you are traveling any significant distance, transport it in a cooler. Keep refrigerated until ready to serve.

· Super Bowl ·
SHINDIG

---— MENU —---

Hold 'em Puffs

Spicy Pita Chips

Chickpea Kickers

Classic Italian Hero

Mole Chili Con Carne

Layered Chopped Salad

Old-Fashioned Popcorn Balls

Apple Crumb Squares

When it comes to the Super Bowl, you can't go wrong with the classics. For nibbles, we've got pop-in-your-mouth Chickpea Kickers and pita chips, as well as a grown-up version of pigs in a blanket, using hearty kielbasa. A layered salad is a crisp counterpoint to the main events, a steaming pot of chili and a homemade party hero. If you've still got room for dessert, there are homey apple squares or chewy-crunchy popcorn balls.

HOLD 'EM PUFFS

ACTIVE TIME 25 minutes · **TOTAL TIME** 40 minutes · **MAKES** 48 puffs

No need to put out mustard for dipping—it's already wrapped in the blanket.

1 Preheat oven to 375°F.

2 Pat kielbasa dry with paper towels. Cut crosswise into ¾-inch-thick rounds; cut each round in half to make half-circles.

3 Unroll half of dough (4 triangles) from tube of crescent rolls but do not separate triangles; place on surface.

4 Pinch 2 triangles together along perforations to make a 6" by 3½" rectangle. Repeat to make another rectangle; cut rectangles apart. Spread with mustard. Cut each rectangle crosswise in half, then cut each half crosswise into six ½-inch-wide strips to make 12 strips from each rectangle.

5 Loosely wrap mustard side of a dough strip around piece of kielbasa; pinch to seal. Place wrapped kielbasa on ungreased large cookie sheet. Repeat, placing pieces about 1 inch apart on cookie sheet. Repeat with remaining half of crescent dough, mustard, and kielbasa.

6 Bake until puffs are browned, 13 to 15 minutes. When puffs are done, with spatula, transfer to warm platter. Serve warm.

1 package (16 ounces) light kielbasa or turkey kielbasa

1 tube (8 ounces) refrigerated crescent rolls

2 tablespoons spicy brown mustard

EACH PUFF
About 40 calories, 2g protein, 2g carbohydrate, 3g total fat (1g saturated), 0g fiber, 6mg cholesterol, 130mg sodium

Hold 'em Puffs, Spicy Pita Chips, and Chickpea Kickers (recipes pages 148–151)

POTLUCK PREP Prepare puffs and set on prepared cookie sheet (you may need 2 sheets to fit them all). Cover with plastic wrap and refrigerate until ready to leave. Have your host preheat her oven so that the puffs can go straight into the oven (after removing the wrap). Get there early enough so the puffs can be coming out of the oven as the other guests arrive.

SPICY PITA CHIPS

ACTIVE TIME 10 minutes · **TOTAL TIME** 18 minutes plus cooling · **MAKES** 8 dozen

Forget the tortilla chips: You can bake these chili- and cumin-scented crisps in a flash. Serve with store-bought hummus topped with a sprinkling of chopped parsley. For photo, see page 149.

1   Preheat oven to 425°F. In 1-cup liquid measuring cup, with fork, mix oil, Parmesan, chili powder, and cumin.

2   With knife or kitchen shears, carefully split each pita. Brush insides of pita halves lightly with oil mixture. Cut each half into 8 wedges.

3   Transfer wedges to 2 ungreased large cookie sheets (wedges can overlap slightly). Place cookie sheets on 2 oven racks and bake chips 8 to 10 minutes or until edges are golden. Watch carefully, as they can burn quickly.

4   Cool chips on cookie sheets on wire racks.

½ cup olive oil

1 tablespoon freshly grated Parmesan or Romano cheese

1 tablespoon chili powder

1 teaspoon ground cumin

1 package (12 ounces) white or whole-wheat pitas

EACH CHIP
About 20 calories, 0g protein, 2g carbohydrate, 1g total fat (0g saturated), 0g fiber, 0mg cholesterol, 20mg sodium

POTLUCK PREP Make chips up to one week before party. Store in a tightly covered container or large self-sealing plastic bag.

CHICKPEA KICKERS

ACTIVE TIME 5 minutes · **TOTAL TIME** 17 minutes
MAKES 1¾ cups or 7 appetizer servings

These little munchies make for fun and unexpected party fare. Provide cocktail picks to make them easy for guests to munch. For photo, see page 149.

1 tablespoon butter or margarine

1 can (15 to 19 ounces) garbanzo beans (chickpeas)

½ teaspoon dried Italian seasoning

¼ teaspoon ground red pepper (cayenne)

¼ teaspoon salt

cocktail picks

1 In nonstick 10-inch skillet, heat butter over medium-high heat until melted and browned, about 5 minutes. Meanwhile, drain and rinse beans. Transfer beans to paper towels; pat completely dry.

2 Add beans, Italian seasoning, ground red pepper, and salt to skillet; cook until beans brown slightly, about 7 minutes, shaking pan occasionally.

3 Transfer beans to shallow bowl. Serve hot or cold with cocktail picks.

EACH ¼ CUP
About 105 calories, 4g protein, 17g carbohydrate, 3g total fat (0g saturated), 3g fiber, 0mg cholesterol, 240mg sodium

POTLUCK PREP Make these snacks right before you leave, then transport in a covered serving bowl.

CLASSIC ITALIAN HERO

TOTAL TIME 15 minutes · **MAKES** 12 servings

Why pay more to buy a giant hero when you can put together your own and tailor it to taste? Whether you call it a hero, sub, hoagie, or grinder, this toothsome sandwich is sure to be a crowd pleaser.

1 Split bread horizontally in half. Remove enough of the soft center from each half to make 1-inch shell. (Reserve soft bread for another use.)

2 Brush vinaigrette evenly over cut sides of bread. Layer meats and cheese on bottom half of bread. Top with additional ingredients of your choice. Replace top half of bread. If not serving right away, wrap sandwich in foil and refrigerate up to 4 hours. Cut in 12 pieces.

1 long loaf (about 16 inches) French or Italian bread (12 ounces)

¼ cup vinaigrette of choice

4 ounces thinly sliced hot and/or sweet capocello, proscuitto, soppressata, and/or salami

4 ounces mozzarella cheese, preferably fresh, thinly sliced

shredded romaine lettuce or arugula

peperoncini, basil leaves, roasted red peppers, very thinly sliced red onions, tapenade, and/or sliced ripe tomatoes

EACH SERVING
About 145 calories, 7g protein, 12g carbohydrate, 8g total fat (2g saturated), 1g fiber, 16mg cholesterol, 408mg sodium

POTLUCK PREP Transport uncut wrapped hero on a baking sheet for support. If transporting it any distance, carry in a cooler, cutting it in half, if necessary, and rewrapping it. Cut into serving pieces at the potluck.

MOLE CHILI CON CARNE

ACTIVE TIME 20 minutes · **BAKE** 1 hour 45 minutes
MAKES 10 main-dish servings

A big pot of hearty chili is just the thing on Super Bowl Sunday. Mole is a rich-tasting, reddish brown sauce containing a surprising ingredient—chocolate—that contributes body without making the sauce sweet.

1 Pat pork and beef dry with paper towels. In 6- to 8-quart Dutch oven, heat oil over medium-high heat until very hot. Add meat in batches and cook until well browned, 5 to 6 minutes, adding more oil if necessary and using slotted spoon to transfer meat to medium bowl as it is browned. (You may need to reduce heat to medium if oil in Dutch oven begins to smoke.) Preheat oven to 325°F.

2 Reduce heat to medium. Add garlic, onions, coriander, cumin, paprika, chipotle chili powder, and cinnamon to drippings in Dutch oven, and cook, stirring frequently, until onion is tender, about 5 minutes.

3 Return meat with its juices to Dutch oven. Stir in beans with their liquid, tomatoes with their juice, water, chocolate, and salt; heat to boiling over high heat, stirring until browned bits are loosened from bottom of Dutch oven.

2 pounds boneless pork shoulder, trimmed and cut into 1-inch pieces

2 pounds boneless beef chuck, trimmed and cut into 1-inch pieces

2 teaspoons vegetable oil

6 garlic cloves, crushed with press

2 medium onions, chopped

1 tablespoon ground coriander

1 tablespoon ground cumin

1 tablespoon paprika

1½ teaspoons chipotle chile powder

½ teaspoon ground cinnamon

3 cans (15 to 19 ounces each) pink beans and/or red kidney beans

1 can (28 ounces) diced tomatoes

1 cup water

2 squares (2 ounces) unsweetened chocolate, chopped

1½ teaspoons salt

warm corn tortillas (optional)

4   Cover and bake until meat is fork-tender, 1 hour and 45 minutes to 2 hours. Skim and discard any fat. Spoon chili into bowls and serve with tortillas, if you like.

EACH SERVING
About 525 calories, 55g protein, 34g carbohydrate, 19g total fat (7g saturated), 13g fiber, 146mg cholesterol, 1,355mg sodium

POTLUCK PREP Heat until bubbling right before leaving. Transfer to a slow cooker to transport; bring a serving ladle. Place on buffet table and set to Keep Warm.

LAYERED CHOPPED SALAD

TOTAL TIME 25 minutes · **MAKES** 22 cups or 16 servings

Serve a crowd with this festive make-ahead salad: Iceberg lettuce and layers of fresh veggies stay crunchy under a creamy blue-cheese dressing until tossed together at serving time. For the prettiest presentation—though it's not essential—serve in a cylindrical clear-glass bowl so that all the colorful layers show up well. In a pinch, you can use a punch bowl or the outer bowl from your salad spinner.

1 Prepare dressing: In small bowl, with fork, mash cheese with milk until creamy. Add mayonnaise, vinegar, mustard, salt, and pepper; mix until blended. Makes about 1¼ cups.

2 Prepare salad: In 6-quart or larger cylindrical clear-glass bowl, place half of lettuce. Top with tomato slices, followed by shredded carrots, remaining lettuce, red peppers, and cucumber slices.

3 Spoon blue-cheese dressing on top. Sprinkle with walnuts. Cover and refrigerate until ready to serve and up to 1 day.

4 Right before serving, toss salad until well coated with dressing.

Creamy Blue-Cheese Dressing

4 ounces blue cheese, crumbled (1 cup)

3 tablespoons milk

½ cup light mayonnaise

2 tablespoons white wine vinegar

1 teaspoon Dijon mustard

⅛ teaspoon salt

⅛ teaspoon coarsely ground black pepper

Salad

1 medium head iceberg lettuce (about 1½ pounds), coarsely chopped

4 medium (about 1¼ pounds) tomatoes, thinly sliced

1 bag (10 ounces) shredded carrots

2 medium red peppers, coarsely chopped

1 English (seedless) cucumber, unpeeled, cut lengthwise in half and thinly sliced crosswise

½ cup walnuts, toasted and chopped

EACH SERVING
About 75 calories, 3g protein, 6g carbohydrate, 5g total fat (2g saturated fat), 2g fiber, 8mg cholesterol, 190mg sodium

POTLUCK PREP Transport in a covered serving bowl. If traveling any distance, carry it in a cooler. Bring two large spoons or salad forks to toss the salad, as well as serving tongs.

OLD-FASHIONED POPCORN BALLS

ACTIVE TIME **30 minutes** · TOTAL TIME **45 minutes** · MAKES **16 popcorn balls**

Get everyone in the spirit for game day!

1 Preheat oven to 350°F. Place pecans and almonds in 17" by 11½" roasting pan; place coconut in 15½" by 10½" jelly-roll pan. Set pans on 2 oven racks and bake nuts and coconut until toasted, 10 to 15 minutes, stirring occasionally. Stir nuts into coconut; cool completely.

2 Line cookie sheet with foil; spray it and roasting pan with nonstick cooking spray. Place popcorn in roasting pan; discard any unpopped kernels. Sprinkle with nut mixture.

3 In heavy saucepan, heat brown sugar, corn syrup, butter, and salt to boiling over medium-high heat, stirring frequently. Reduce heat to medium; boil 5 minutes. Remove saucepan from heat; stir in vanilla and baking soda. Very carefully, pour hot caramel syrup over popcorn mixture; toss with 2 forks until evenly coated.

4 Working quickly, scoop up hot popcorn mixture by level cups and place on prepared cookie sheet. When cool enough to handle, coat hands with cooking spray; shape mounds into balls, pressing lightly so they hold together. Cool completely.

1 cup pecans

1 cup sliced almonds

1½ cups flaked sweetened coconut

16 cups popped corn (from about ¾ cup unpopped kernels)

1¼ cups packed brown sugar

1¼ cups dark corn syrup

6 tablespoons butter or margarine

½ teaspoon salt

½ teaspoon vanilla extract

¼ teaspoon baking soda

EACH POPCORN BALL
About 330 calories, 3g protein, 48g carbohydrate, 16g total fat (6g saturated), 32g fiber, 12mg cholesterol, 180mg sodium

POTLUCK PREP Wrap each ball in plastic wrap. Store in tightly covered container at room temperature up to 1 week. Bring to the party in a decorative basket.

APPLE CRUMB SQUARES

ACTIVE TIME 1 hour · **TOTAL TIME** 2 hours plus cooling · **MAKES** 24 squares

These luscious squares combine all the flavors of a streusel-topped apple pie without the rolling.

1 Prepare crumb topping: In medium bowl, with fingertips, mix all topping ingredients until mixture comes together. Shape into a ball; wrap in plastic wrap and refrigerate until ready to use.

2 Preheat oven to 375°F. Lightly grease sides of 15½" by 10½" jelly-roll pan.

3 Prepare crust: In large bowl, with fork, mix flour, granulated sugar, and salt. With pastry blender or 2 knives used scissors-fashion, blend butter into flour mixture until mixture resembles fine crumbs. With hand, press fine-crumb mixture evenly into bottom of prepared pan. Bake crust until golden brown (it may crack slightly), 20 to 24 minutes.

4 Meanwhile, prepare apple filling: In nonstick 12-inch skillet, cook apples, butter, raisins, brown sugar, and cinnamon over medium heat until apples are very tender and most liquid from apples evaporates, 25 to 30 minutes, stirring occasionally. In cup, mix cornstarch and lemon juice. Stir lemon-juice

Crumb Topping

1 cup all-purpose flour

1 cup pecans or walnuts, coarsely chopped

½ cup butter or margarine (1 stick), slightly softened

½ cup packed brown sugar

1 tablespoon vanilla extract

1 teaspoon ground cinnamon

Crust

3 cups all-purpose flour

⅓ cup granulated sugar

¼ teaspoon salt

¾ cup cold butter or margarine (1½ sticks)

mixture into apple mixture and cook until mixture thickens, stirring. Remove skillet from heat.

5   Spread apple mixture over hot crust. Break chilled crumb topping into chunks and scatter over apple mixture. Bake until topping browns, about 40 minutes. Cool completely in pan on wire rack.

6   To serve, cut lengthwise into 4 strips, then cut each strip crosswise into 6 squares.

Apple Filling

4 pounds green apples, such as Granny Smith, peeled, cored, and cut into ½-inch chunks

4 tablespoons butter or margarine

¾ cup raisins or dried currants

½ cup packed brown sugar

¾ teaspoon ground cinnamon

1 tablespoon plus 2 teaspoons cornstarch

3 tablespoons fresh lemon juice

EACH SQUARE
About 315 calories, 3g protein, 42g carbohydrate, 16g total fat (8g saturated), 3g fiber, 33mg cholesterol, 155mg sodium

POTLUCK PREP   Transport squares in a cookie tin, separating layers with waxed paper, or piled decoratively on a serving plate.

· Midwinter ·
BLUES BASH

MENU

Tomato-Basil Cream
Cheese Logs

Roasted Asparagus

Slow-Cooker Short Ribs with
Root Vegetables

Hungarian Veal Goulash

Scalloped Potatoes with
Green Onions

Apple Upside-Down
Bread Pudding

It's mid-February, the holidays are long gone, and you haven't seen the sun in days. How to raise your flagging spirits? Plan a potluck with the spotlight on comfort foods and banish those midwinter blues! For a starter, have a guest prepare our cheese logs, packed with dried tomatoes and basil, the flavors of summer. For entrées, we've got meaty dishes that will have guests sighing with contentment. You can serve them both with a big bowl of buttered egg noodles or our scalloped potatoes. Roasted asparagus, with its charry flavor reminiscent of grilling, will remind everyone that spring is on its way. For a sweet finale, sit back and enjoy a delicious old-fashioned bread pudding studded with apples.

TOMATO-BASIL CREAM CHEESE LOGS

TOTAL TIME 15 minutes plus soaking and chilling
MAKES two 6-inch logs or 24 servings

Bursting with bright flavors, this cream cheese log may be spread on thinly sliced and toasted Italian bread or crackers. To toast the pine nuts, place them in a dry skillet over low heat until lightly browned (3 to 5 minutes), shaking or stirring often.

1 Soak dried tomatoes in enough *boiling water* to cover until softened, about 15 minutes. Drain tomatoes well, then finely chop.

2 In small bowl, with mixer on medium speed, beat cream cheese until light and creamy, about 1 minute. Stir in drained tomatoes, basil, Parmesan, and pepper.

3 On waxed paper, shape half of cheese mixture into 6-inch-long log; roll up in waxed paper. Repeat with remaining cheese mixture.

4 Refrigerate until chilled and firm, at least 1 hour.

5 Roll logs in pine nuts; wrap and chill 15 minutes longer.

1/3 cup dried tomatoes

2 packages (8 ounces each) cream cheese, softened

1/3 cup chopped fresh basil

1/4 cup freshly grated Parmesan cheese

1/2 teaspoon coarsely ground black pepper

1/2 cup pine nuts (pignoli), toasted and finely chopped

EACH SERVING
About 90 calories, 3g protein, 2g carbohydrate, 8g total fat (5g saturated), 0g fiber, 22mg cholesterol, 76mg sodium

POTLUCK PREP Prepare far enough in advance to allow proper chilling. Bring two serving plates large enough to accommodate a cheese log and crackers or toasts and two serving knives. If using toasted Italian bread, toast ahead of time and bring in a zip-tight plastic bag. Or bring a box of crackers (or several different kinds, if you like).

ROASTED ASPARAGUS

ACTIVE TIME 5 minutes · **TOTAL TIME** About 15 minutes
MAKES 8 side-dish servings

For a recipe that is so astonishingly simple, it delivers incredible flavor. No matter how much you make, you'll never have leftovers.

1 Preheat oven to 450°F.

2 In 15½" by 10½" jelly-roll pan, sprinkle asparagus with salt and pepper and drizzle with oil; shake pan to coat asparagus. Roast asparagus until lightly browned and tender, 10 to 12 minutes (depending on thickness). Remove pan from oven; cover with foil to keep warm.

3 Just before serving, transfer the asparagus to a serving platter and sprinkle with the Parmesan.

2 bunches asparagus (about 2 pounds), trimmed

½ teaspoon salt

½ teaspoon coarsely ground black pepper

2 tablespoons olive oil

¼ cup freshly grated Parmesan cheese

EACH SERVING
About 55 calories, 2g protein, 3g carbohydrate, 4g total fat (1g saturated), 1g fiber, 2mg cholesterol, 195mg sodium

POTLUCK PREP Since this is an entirely last-minute dish, we recommend that the host prepare this dish.

SLOW-COOKER SHORT RIBS WITH ROOT VEGETABLES

ACTIVE TIME 35 minutes · **TOTAL TIME** 8½ hours on Low or 4½ hours on High
MAKES 6 main-dish servings

Short ribs were made for the slow cooker, long, low cooking transforming them into delectably rich tenderness. Look for the meatiest ribs you can find.

1 Heat 12-inch skillet over medium-high heat until hot. Add ribs to skillet and sprinkle with ½ teaspoon salt and ¼ teaspoon pepper. Cook until well browned on all sides, about 10 minutes, turning occasionally.

2 Meanwhile, in 5- to 6-quart slow-cooker pot, place parsnips, turnip, and carrots.

3 Transfer ribs to slow cooker on top of vegetables. Discard drippings in skillet. Reduce heat to medium; add onion to skillet and cook until browned, about 8 minutes, stirring frequently. Add garlic and thyme and cook 1 minute, stirring constantly. Add wine and heat to boiling over high heat, stirring to loosen browned bits from bottom of skillet. Remove skillet from heat and stir in tomato

3 pounds bone-in beef chuck short ribs

1 teaspoon salt

½ teaspoon ground black pepper

2 large parsnips (4 ounces each), peeled and cut into 1-inch chunks

1 medium turnip (8 ounces), peeled and cut into 1-inch chunks

1 bag (16 ounces) peeled baby carrots

1 jumbo onion (1 pound), coarsely chopped

4 large garlic cloves, thinly sliced

1 teaspoon dried thyme

2 cups dry red wine

¼ cup tomato paste

POTLUCK PREP Finish cooking or reheat to serving temperature right before leaving. Transport to potluck in the slow cooker, along with serving platter and tongs. Plug cooker in and set to Keep Warm. When ready to serve, transfer short ribs and vegetables to platter as directed in step 5.

paste and remaining ½ teaspoon salt and ¼ teaspoon pepper.

4 Pour wine mixture over ribs in slow cooker. Cover slow cooker with lid and cook on Low setting as manufacturer directs, 8 to 10 hours (or on High setting 4 to 5 hours) or until meat is fork-tender and falling off the bones.

5 With tongs, transfer ribs to deep platter; discard bones if you like. With spoon, skim fat from sauce in slow cooker and discard fat. Spoon vegetables and sauce over ribs.

EACH SERVING
About 655 calories, 27g protein, 24g carbohydrate, 50g total fat (21g saturated), 5g fiber, 114mg cholesterol, 535mg sodium

HUNGARIAN VEAL GOULASH

ACTIVE TIME 45 minutes · **TOTAL TIME** 2 hours · **MAKES** 8 main-dish servings

Goulash is another luxurious midwinter indulgence, with its deliciously tender veal.

1 In 5- to 6-quart Dutch oven, heat oil over medium-high heat until very hot but not smoking. Add one-third of veal and cook until browned, 8 to 10 minutes, turning occasionally. With slotted spoon, transfer veal, as it browns, to bowl. Repeat with remaining veal in 2 more batches.

2 Preheat oven to 350°F.

3 To same Dutch oven, add onion and cook over medium heat until browned, about 6 minutes, stirring frequently. Stir in garlic, paprika, caraway seeds, salt, and pepper; cook 1 minute, stirring constantly.

4 Return veal and any juices to Dutch oven. Stir in sauerkraut, tomatoes with their juice, broth, and water; heat to boiling over high heat, stirring to loosen browned bits from bottom of Dutch oven. Cover Dutch oven and place in oven. Bake goulash until veal is tender, about 1 hour 15 minutes.

5 Just before serving, stir in sour cream.

1 tablespoon vegetable oil

2½ pounds boneless veal shoulder roast, trimmed and cut into 1½-inch chunks

1 large onion (12 ounces), coarsely chopped

2 large garlic cloves, crushed with garlic press

3 tablespoons paprika, preferably sweet Hungarian

¼ teaspoon caraway seeds

½ teaspoon salt

¼ teaspoon ground black pepper

1 bag (16 ounces) sauerkraut, rinsed and well drained

1 can (14½ ounces) diced tomatoes

1 can (14½ ounces) reduced-sodium beef broth (1¾ cups)

¾ cup water

½ cup light sour cream

EACH SERVING
About 230 calories, 32g protein, 9g carbohydrate, 7g total fat (2g saturated), 3g fiber, 123mg cholesterol, 725mg sodium

POTLUCK PREP Bake dish right before leaving. Transport in Dutch oven in an insulated food carrier. You could also transfer and transport in a slow cooker. Bring serving ladle. Stir sour cream into goulash just before serving.

SCALLOPED POTATOES WITH GREEN ONIONS

ACTIVE TIME 30 minutes · **TOTAL TIME** 1 hour 45 minutes · **MAKES** 12 side-dish servings

The creamy smoothness of these potatoes is a perfect pairing with the ribs and goulash.

1 Preheat oven to 400°F. Lightly grease 13" by 9" glass or ceramic baking dish or 2½-quart gratin dish.

2 In 6-quart saucepot, melt butter over medium heat. Thinly slice green onions, reserving 2 tablespoons green tops. Add sliced green onions to pot; cook until tender, about 5 minutes, stirring often. Add flour; cook, stirring, 1 minute. With wire whisk, gradually whisk in milk. Cook over medium heat until mixture boils and thickens, 6 to 7 minutes, stirring constantly. Stir in potatoes, salt, and pepper. Cook 5 minutes, stirring; remove from heat.

3 Transfer potato mixture to prepared baking dish, spreading evenly; sprinkle with Parmesan. Cover with foil sprayed with nonstick cooking spray; bake 1 hour.

4 Uncover dish; reset oven control to broil. Broil, 6 inches from heat source, until Parmesan is golden, about 5 minutes. Sprinkle with reserved green onions and serve.

3 tablespoons butter or margarine

1 bunch green onions

3 tablespoons all-purpose flour

2¼ cups milk

4 pounds all-purpose potatoes, peeled and thinly sliced

1 teaspoon salt

½ teaspoon ground black pepper

½ cup freshly grated Parmesan cheese

EACH SERVING
About 195 calories, 6g protein, 31g carbohydrate, 6g total fat (2.5g saturated), 2g fiber, 10mg cholesterol, 323mg sodium

POTLUCK PREP Prepare through step 3 right before leaving. Transport in an insulated food carrier. Bring serving spoon and reserved green onions in zip-tight plastic bag. At potluck, run the potatoes under the broiler and sprinkle with green onions as directed in step 4.

APPLE UPSIDE-DOWN BREAD PUDDING

ACTIVE TIME 40 minutes · **TOTAL TIME** 2 hours 40 minutes, plus chilling

MAKES 12 servings

It may look homely, but bread pudding is always a winner at any sort of get-together.

1 In medium bowl, with wire whisk, mix eggs, cinnamon, nutmeg, and 6 tablespoons granulated sugar until sugar dissolves. Add milk, cream, Calvados, and 1½ teaspoons vanilla; whisk until combined.

2 Place bread in large bowl. Pour milk mixture over bread; cover and refrigerate at least 1½ hours or overnight, occasionally pressing bread down to absorb milk mixture.

3 Meanwhile, in nonstick 12-inch skillet, melt 4 tablespoons butter over medium heat. Stir in brown sugar, remaining 6 tablespoons granulated sugar, and remaining 1 tablespoon vanilla. Add apples and cook until tender and syrup thickens and turns a deep caramel color, 18 to 22 minutes, turning apples occasionally.

4 Preheat oven to 325°F. Fill kettle or covered 4-quart saucepan with *water*; heat to boiling over high heat.

6 large eggs

1 tablespoon ground cinnamon

1½ teaspoons ground nutmeg

¾ cup granulated sugar

2½ cups milk

1 cup heavy or whipping cream

2 tablespoons Calvados (apple brandy; optional)

1½ teaspoons plus 1 tablespoon vanilla extract

6 cups 1-inch cubes dry white bread (from 10- to 12-ounce loaf; see Tip, opposite)

5 tablespoons butter

½ cup packed brown sugar

4 Granny Smith apples, peeled, cored, and each cut into quarters

POTLUCK PREP Bake right before leaving; transport in an insulated food carrier. Don't bother to let it stand; it'll lose too much heat. Bring a server and platter and unmold right before serving.

5 Place apples, rounded sides down, in deep 3-quart glass or ceramic baking dish. Pour bread mixture over apples. Cut remaining tablespoon butter into small cubes and sprinkle over pudding. Place baking dish in large roasting pan and cover dish with foil; place on rack in center of oven. Carefully pour *boiling water* into roasting pan to come halfway up sides of baking dish. Bake pudding 1 hour 30 minutes.

6 Uncover and bake until knife inserted 1 inch from center of pudding comes out clean, about 30 minutes longer. Let stand 15 minutes to allow pudding to set slightly. To unmold, run knife around sides of baking dish; place platter on top of baking dish then invert both, allowing syrup to drip from dish. Serve warm.

EACH SERVING
About 350 calories, 7g protein, 41g carbohydrate, 18g total fat (10g saturated), 2g fiber, 154mg cholesterol, 215mg sodium

TIP To dry out bread, preheat oven to 325°F. Place bread in 15½" by 10½" jelly-roll pan or large cookie sheet. Toast bread until golden, 30 to 35 minutes, stirring halfway through toasting. Cool bread in pan on wire racks.

Metric Equivalent Charts

The recipes in this book use the standard U.S. method for measuring liquid and dry or solid ingredients (teaspoons, tablespoons, and cups). The information on this chart is provided to help cooks outside the Unites States successfully use these recipes. All equivalents are approximate.

METRIC EQUIVALENTS FOR DIFFERENT TYPES OF INGREDIENTS

A standard cup measure of a dry or solid ingredient will vary in weight depending on the type of ingredient. A standard cup of liquid is the same volume for any type of liquid. Use the following chart when converting standard cup measures to grams (weight) or milliliters (volume).

STANDARD CUP	FINE POWDER (E.G., FLOUR)	GRAIN (E.G., RICE)	GRANULAR (E.G., SUGAR)	LIQUID SOLIDS (E.G., BUTTER)	LIQUID (E.G., MILK)
1	140g	150g	190g	200g	240ml
3/4	105g	113g	143g	150g	180ml
2/3	93g	100g	125g	133g	160ml
1/2	70g	75g	95g	100g	120ml
1/3	47g	50g	63g	67g	80ml
1/4	35g	38g	48g	50g	60ml
1/8	18g	19g	24g	25g	30ml

USEFUL EQUIVALENTS FOR DRY INGREDIENTS BY WEIGHT
(To convert ounces to grams, multiply the number of ounces by 30.)

1 oz	=	3/16 lb	=	30g
4 oz	=	1/4 lb	=	120g
8 oz	=	1/2 lb	=	240g
12 oz	=	3/4 lb	=	360g
16 oz	=	1 lb	=	480g

USEFUL EQUIVALENTS FOR
LIQUID INGREDIENTS BY VOLUME

¼ tsp			=			1ml		
½ tsp			=			2ml		
1 tsp			=			5ml		
3 tsp	=	1 tblsp	=	½ fl oz	=	15ml		
2 tblsp	=	⅛ cup	=	1 fl oz	=	30ml		
4 tblsp	=	¼ cup	=	2 fl oz	=	60ml		
5⅓ tblsp	=	⅓ cup	=	3 fl oz	=	80ml		
8 tblsp	=	½ cup	=	4 fl oz	=	120ml		
10⅔ tblsp	=	⅔ cup	=	5 fl oz	=	160ml		
12 tblsp	=	¾ cup	=	6 fl oz	=	180ml		
16 tblsp	=	1 cup	=	8 fl oz	=	240ml		
1 pt	=	2 cups	=	16 fl oz	=	480ml		
1 qt	=	4 cups	=	32 fl oz	=	960ml		
				33 fl oz	=	1000ml	=	1 L

USEFUL EQUIVALENTS FOR
COOKING/OVEN TEMPERATURES

	FARENHEIT	CELCIUS	GAS MARK
FREEZE WATER	32°F	0°C	
ROOM TEMPERATURE	68°F	20°C	
BOIL WATER	212°F	100°C	
BAKE	325°F	160°C	3
	350°F	180°C	4
	375°F	190°C	5
	400°F	200°C	6
	425°F	220°C	7
	450°F	230°C	8
BROIL			Grill

Index

Photography Credits

Front Cover (clockwise from top left): Tara Donne, Mark Thomas, Monica Buck, Mark Thomas

Spine: Frances Janisch

Back Cover (from top left): Frances Janisch, James Baigrie, Rita Maas

Antonis Achilleos: 34 middle right, 43, 160 bottom left, 171

James Baigrie: 4, 9, 13, 14, 18 top right, 18 middle left, 18 bottom left, 25, 26, 29, 34 top left and bottom right, 44, 47, 50 middle right, 58, 70 bottom middle, 77, 86 top right, 90, 116 top left, 116 bottom right, 123, 132 center and bottom left, 138, 141, 146 bottom middle and right, 149, 160 center, 168

Mary Ellen Bartley: 132 top right, 137

Monica Buck: 98 bottom middle, 111

Beatriz Da Costa: 132 top left and bottom right, 145

Tara Donne: 34 middle left, 37, 70 top left, 75, 116 middle left and right, 116 bottom right, 124, 127, 128

Getty Images: Ann Cutting: 50 bottom right; Victoria Firmston: 86 middle left; Brian Hagiwara: 146 top middle; Louise Lister: 98 bottom left, 109; Jean Maurice: 10, Rob Tringali: 146 middle right

Thayer Allyson Gowdy: 70 center, 72

Brian Hagiwara: 70 middle right

Lisa Hubbard: 18 bottom middle, 33, 86 top left, 97

iStockphoto: 132 top middle; Pattie Calfy: 116 bottom middle, 160 bottom middle; Jill Chen: 7; Jodie Coston: 70 bottom right; Anne Cutler: 50 bottom left; Jennifer Daley: 86 top middle; Steve Debenport: 34 top right; Larysa Dodz: 160 middle left; Alan Egginton: 160 bottom right; Elena Elisseeva: 132 bottom middle; Evelin Elmest: 18 center; Lyle Gregg: 70 top middle; Carly Hennigan: 34 bottom left; Jim Jurica: 50 center; Nils Kahle: 160 middle right; Sean Locke: 17, 98 center, 98 bottom right; Patricia Nelson: 132 middle left; John Peacock: 98 top middle, 104; Dawn Poland: 132 middle right; Andrew Rich: 70 middle left, 146 bottom left; Eva Serrabassa: 86 bottom right; David Sischo: 34 center; Mark Swallow: 86 middle right; Christopher Walker: 160 top middle; Mark Wragg: 18 top left and bottom right

Frances Janisch: 34 top middle, 34 bottom middle, 40, 49, 70 top right, 80, 81, 98 middle right, 106, 160 top left and right, 165, 166

Rita Maas: 18 top middle, 18 middle right, 23, 31, 50 top left and top right, 53, 54, 98 top right, 98 middle left, 101, 115, 116 center, 118, 135 (both photos)

Kate Mathis: 98 top left, 105

Andrew McCaul: 70 bottom left

Alan Richardson: 50 middle left, 62

Ann Stratton: 86 bottom left, 86 bottom middle, 89, 94, 116 bottom left, 131, 146 top right, 146 middle left, 155, 159

Studio D: Philip Friedman: 5

Mark Thomas: 6, 50 top middle, 50 bottom middle, 64, 116 top middle, 121, 146 center, 153

James Worrell: 86 center, 93

· Dress Up Your ·
TABLE

———————————•———————————

Decorate your potluck buffet with these festive table-tent cards. We've provided space for you to fill in the name of the dish and who prepared it, along with a checklist of ingredients that might be problematic for some of your guests. Choose from four different color schemes to match your event.

———————————•———————————

HERE'S HOW TO ASSEMBLE THEM:

Tear out the card along the perforated line.

•

Fold along the white lines to create the tents.

•

Tape the flaps at the bottom to secure them.

O Vegetarian   O Contains dairy   O Contains nuts   O Contains wheat products

FROM THE KITCHEN OF

.... *Recipe* ....

.... *Recipe* ....

FROM THE KITCHEN OF

O Vegetarian   O Contains dairy   O Contains nuts   O Contains wheat products